My Big Book of Transport

First published in Great Britain in 2002 by Brimax™.
This paperback edition first published in Great Britain in 2003 by Brimax
An imprint of Octopus Publishing Group Ltd
2-4 Heron Quays, London E14 4JP

A CIP catalogue record for this book is available from the British Library.

Created by

Tall Tree Ltd

ISBN 1 85854 550 1 (hardback)
ISBN 1 85854 8446 (paperback)

Printed in China

My Big Book of Transport

Written by Jon Richards

Illustrated by David Leeks

BRIMAX

Contents

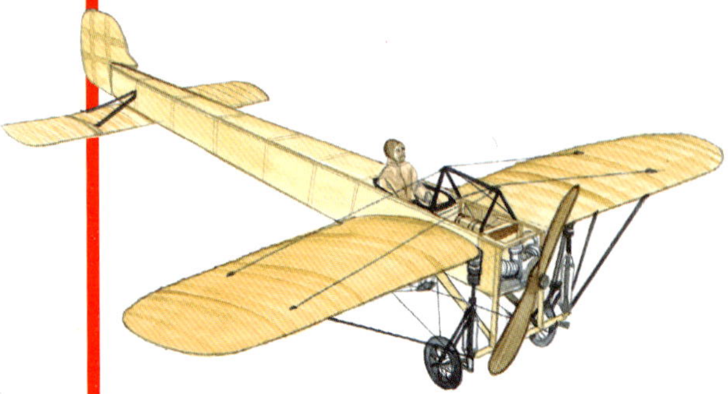

Early land travel 6

The wheel 8

Trains and trams 10

Cars 12

Trucks 14

Weird and wonderful 16

Future land travel 18

Early sea travel 20

Sails and oars 22

Paddles and propellers 24

Other boats 26

Submarines 28

Future sea travel 30

Early flight 32

Balloons and airships 34

Biplanes and triplanes 36

Propeller power 38

Jets 40

Helicopters 42

Space and the future 44

Glossary 46

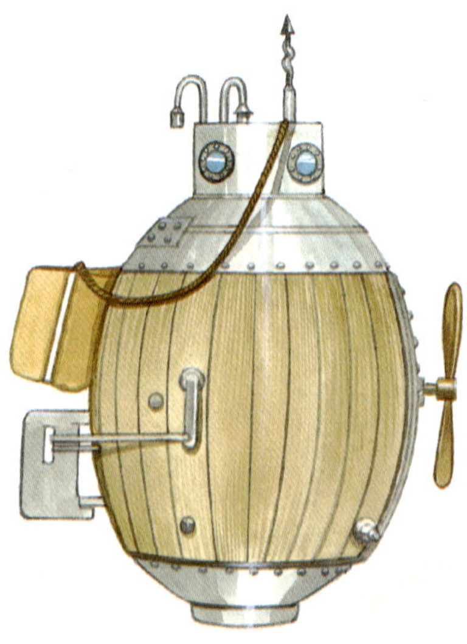

Introduction

Can you imagine a world without any transport? There would not be any cars, trucks, or buses to carry us about. We would not be able to cross rivers and oceans because there would be no boats and ships. Without any planes we would not be able to fly around the world, and astronauts could not go into space without any rockets.

This book will show you the huge range of vehicles that people have built to travel about in, from carts and crawlers, to rafts and rockets. Each topic is explained simply and supported by bright illustrations, amazing facts, and easy-to-understand descriptions of how these machines work.

Early land travel

Long before the invention of the wheel, people still needed to move from place to place to find food and somewhere to live. The only forms of transport available were their own feet or a tame animal.

Around the world on foot

Before people had tamed animals, they had to travel around on foot. Despite this, some were able to leave Africa, where humans are said to have evolved, and populate all parts of the globe.

Sleigh

One of the simplest vehicles is the sleigh. It doesn't have wheels, but it does have two runners along which it is dragged.

Did you know?

The Incas ruled an empire that stretched over 2,200 miles (3,520 kilometres), and all without inventing the wheel!

Pack animals

For thousands of years, people around the world have trained animals to carry loads or to work for them. These include dogs, which can carry small packs or drag light loads, oxen, llamas, and even enormous elephants, which can lift whole trees with their bendy trunks.

Litter

Rich people did not have to walk around everywhere. They paid people to carry them around. Royalty and noble people used to have teams of servants who carried them around in a comfortable box, called a litter.

A litter had arms which rested on the servants' shoulders.

Elephants are the largest and strongest animals on land. This makes them ideal for carrying heavy loads.

How it works

The camel is the perfect mode of transport for crossing a desert. It has large feet which spread with each step to stop it from sinking into the sand and long eyelashes to stop sand from blowing into its eyes. It also has a large hump in which it stores water. This means that it can go for long periods between drinks.

The wheel

The wheel was invented over 6,000 years ago and has been called the greatest invention ever. It has been fitted on many different vehicles, including chariots, coaches, and bicycles.

Chariots

A chariot was a fast, open vehicle that was used for warfare or racing. It could be pulled by two or more horses, but sometimes as many as ten were used.

Rickshaw

Some eastern societies used small, two-wheeled carriages that were pulled by people. They were called rickshaws. Many are still in use today.

Coaches and carriages

Coaches and carriages came in many shapes and sizes, including models with two wheels, such as a Hansom cab, or four wheels, such as a landau. Perhaps the most famous were the stagecoaches which carried people and sometimes the mail over long distances. These large vehicles proved very tempting targets for robbers, known as highwaymen.

How it works

The wheel is one of the simplest machines ever invented. The round disc that makes up the wheel has a rod, called the axle, pushed through its middle. This lets the wheel spin around, rather than drag along the ground. This reduces friction and allows the vehicle to move easily.

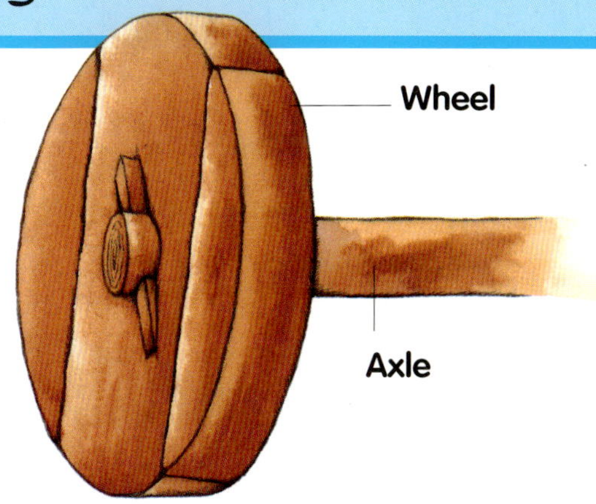

Did you know?

Chariots were not always pulled by horses. Sometimes, people used dogs, camels, and even ostriches!

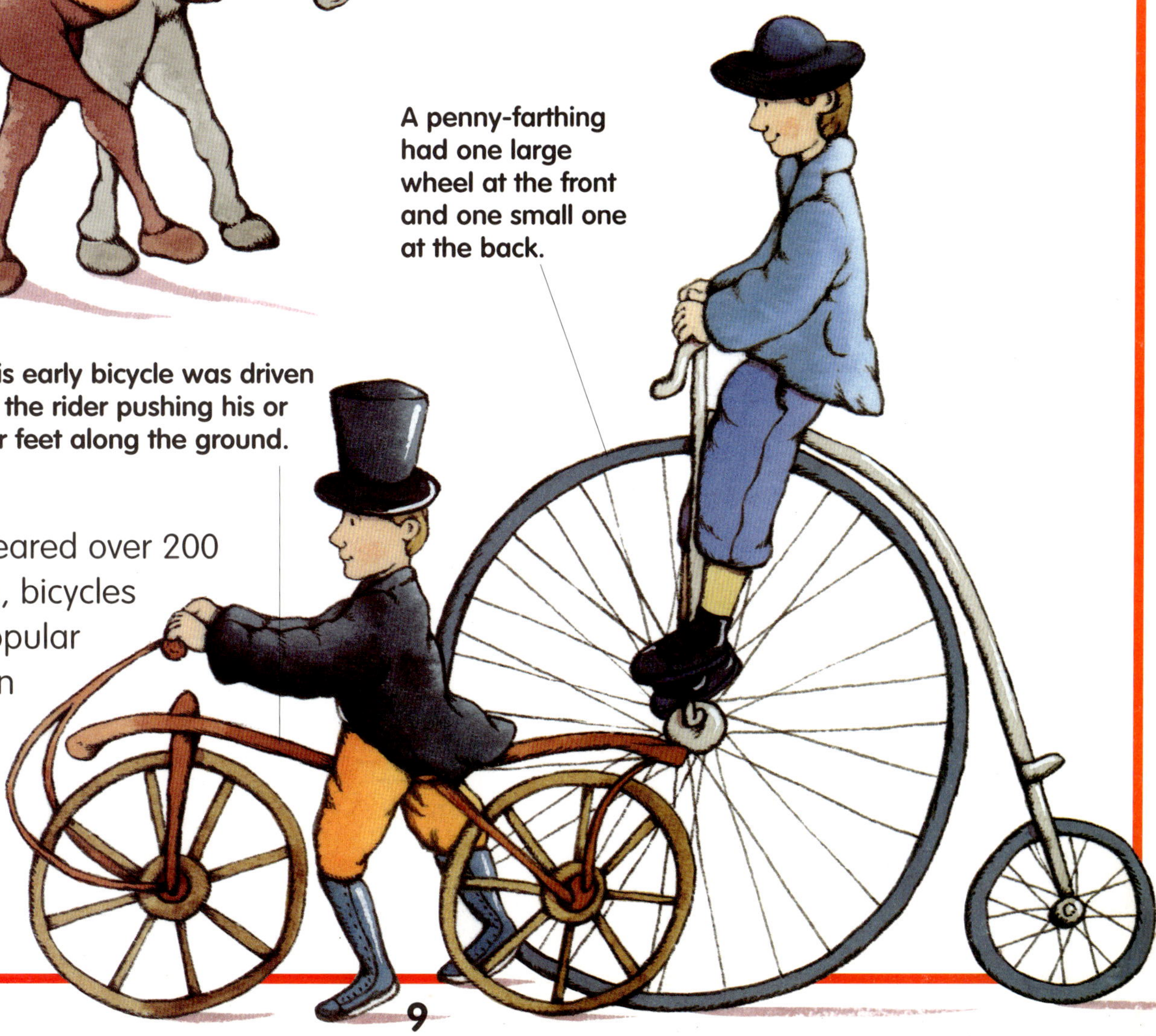

A penny-farthing had one large wheel at the front and one small one at the back.

This early bicycle was driven by the rider pushing his or her feet along the ground.

Bicycles

The first bicycles appeared over 200 years ago. Since then, bicycles have become very popular and have been built in many shapes and sizes, including penny-farthings, racing bikes, and mountain bikes.

Trains and trams

The earliest trains were built nearly 500 years ago. These were wooden vehicles pulled along tracks by horses. The first steam-powered locomotives were built just over 200 years ago. Today, trains are pulled by electric and diesel locomotives and can reach speeds of 480 km/h (300 mph).

Wild west train

This steam train was used a lot in America nearly 200 years ago. It was called a 4-4-0 because it had four small wheels at the front, four larger wheels behind these, and no other wheels at the rear.

Locomotion

This locomotive was one of the first ever built. It started work in 1825, carrying people and cargo between the British industrial towns of Stockton and Darlington.

Trams

Like trains, trams run on rails. However, a tram's rails are set into the streets of a town or city. Modern trams are powered by electricity which they pick up from overhead cables using a springy device called a pantograph.

How it works

Steam trains work by heating up water until it boils and forms steam. The pressure from this steam is then used to push pistons backwards and forwards. These pistons then turn the wheels of the train.

Underground trains

Many large cities have their own underground rail networks. These trains are powered by electricity which is carried along a third rail.

Did you know?

The wheels on the largest locomotive, the Big Boy, were as tall as an adult.

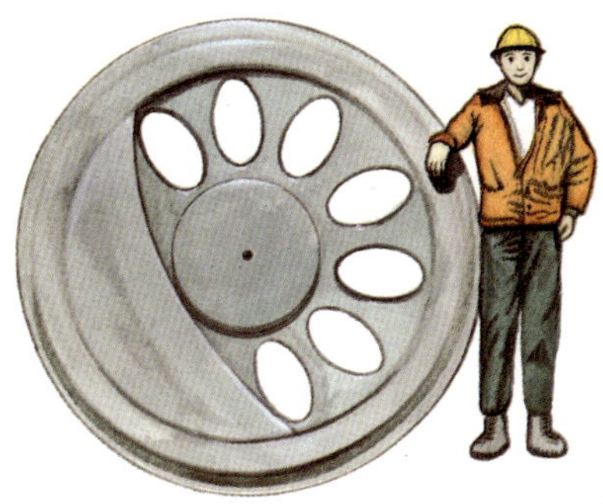

Monorail

A monorail is a special type of train which runs on just one rail. The train can either sit on the single track or it can can hang underneath.

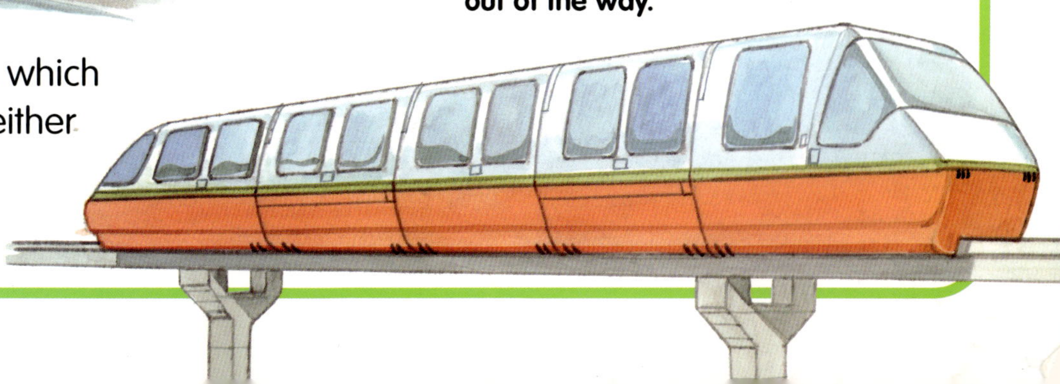

Cars

Today, there are millions of cars on our streets. They can zoom along very quickly and can carry people for hundreds of miles. Modern cars are very different from the earliest vehicles that took to our roads.

Steam carriage

This very early "car" was built in 1769 by French engineer, Nicholas-Joseph Cugenot. It was powered by a steam engine and was designed to pull cannons around a battlefield.

How it works

An internal combustion engine works by mixing fuel and air in a cylinder. This mixture is then squeezed by a piston and set alight. The explosion forces the piston down. This movement ultimately turns the wheels around and moves the car forward.

These wings create a force called "downforce". This helps the racing car stick to the road.

The engine on this racing car sits behind the driver.

Ford Model T

This car was introduced in 1908 and is one of the most popular cars ever built. It was also the first car to be built using a production line in a factory.

Racing cars

There are many different types of racing cars. Some have only one driver and have very streamlined bodies with wings. Others may have a driver and co-driver and need to be very strong to cope with cross-country rally driving.

Did you know?

For early cars, the speed limit was 6.5 km/h (4 mph). Also, a person had to walk in front of the car carrying a red flag to warn other road users.

Choosing a car

Cars come in many shapes and sizes. They can be sports cars that can go very fast, but only carry two people, large off-road utility vehicles, or comfortable family cars.

Family cars usually have a large boot to carry lots of luggage.

Thrust SSC

This car broke the world land speed record and was the first car to travel faster than the speed of sound. It reached a top speed of 1,221 km/h (763 mph).

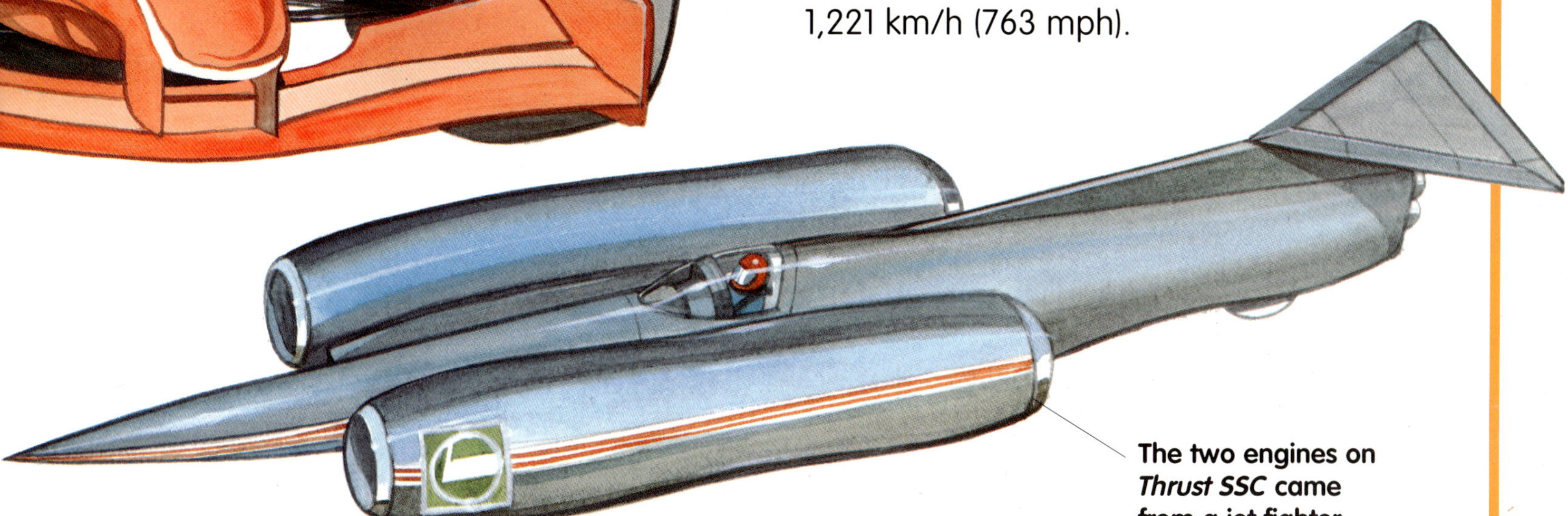

The two engines on *Thrust SSC* came from a jet fighter.

Trucks

The roads today are full of trucks in all shapes and sizes. These huge vehicles pull heavy loads, and can carry tools which lift objects, dig holes, or mix concrete.

Articulated trucks

At the front of a long truck is the tractor unit where the driver sits and the engine roars. The tractor unit pulls along a trailer which holds the load. This type of truck is called an articulated truck because it can bend in the middle.

Old trucks

Old trucks had very little shelter for their drivers. Anyone sitting in the cab had no roof or windscreen to protect them from any bad weather.

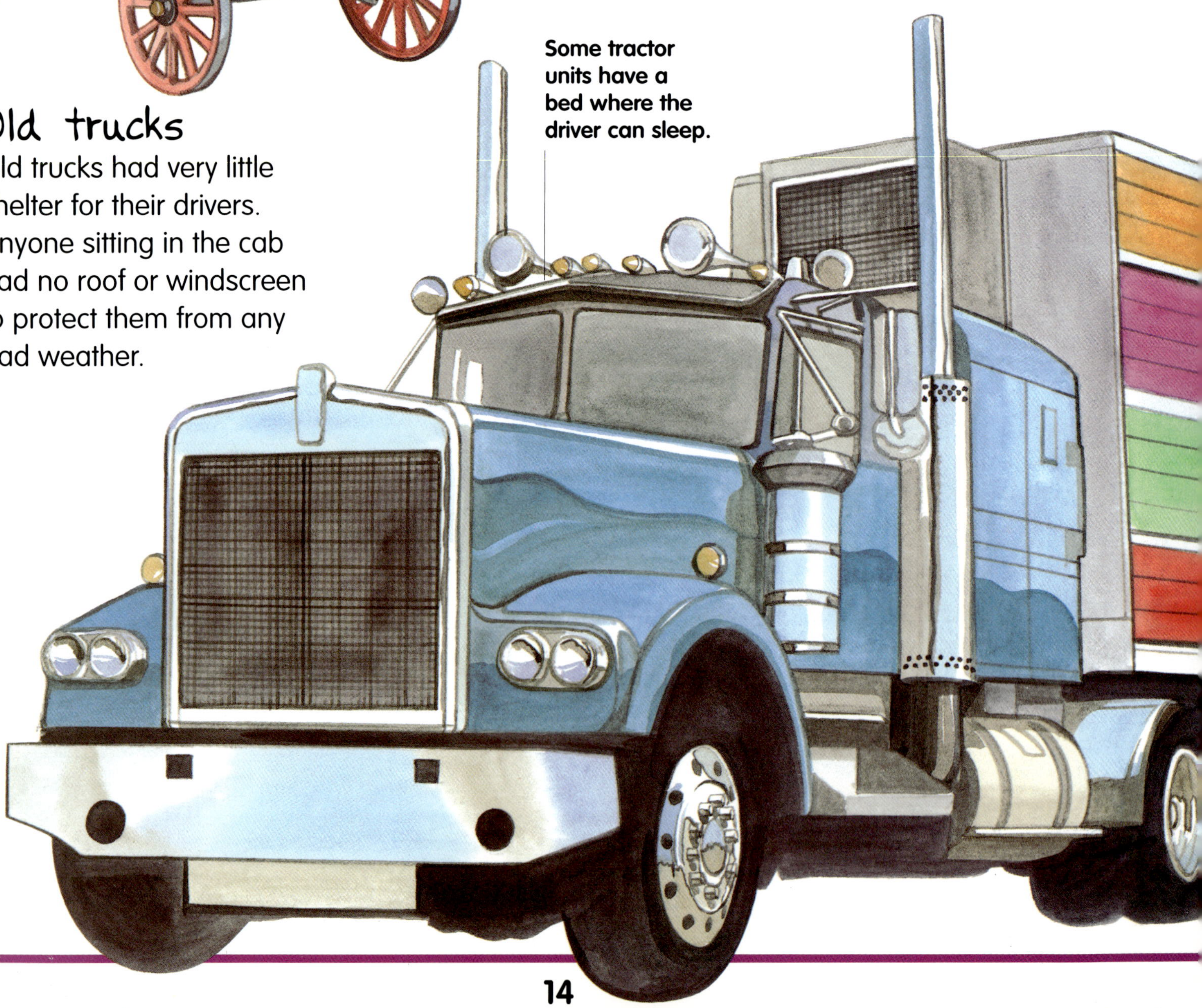

How it works

The tyres on off-road trucks and tractors have a deep pattern carved into them. This is called a tread. The tread helps the vehicle to get a better grip in muddy conditions and stops the truck from sliding around.

Road train

In Australia, some tractor units pull three, four, or even five trailers. These very long trucks are called road trains.

This tractor has small front wheels and large rear wheels.

Large trucks have a lot of wheels to support the weight of the load.

Tractor

Tractors are used to do many jobs around the farm. They can lift bales of hay or pull along different pieces of equipment, including rollers and seed drills.

Did you know?

The fastest truck in the world was fitted with three jet-fighter engines. It reached a speed of 256 mph (412 km/h).

Weird and wonderful

There are a great many other types of land vehicles that are used for a whole range of purposes. Some of them are used to race, some can swim, and some have even gone to the Moon!

Drag tractor

Drag tractor racing is the most powerful motor sport. Special tractors compete to see who can pull a heavy load the furthest.

Swimming truck

This strange looking truck can actually swim! Its body is waterproof and there is a propeller at the back to push it through the water. Trucks like this were used during World War II. They could carry 30 soldiers and swim through water at 6 mph (10 km/h).

Did you know?

The three Lunar Rovers that were taken to the Moon were all left there.

ATV

All Terrain Vehicles, or ATVs, are small, four-wheeled machines that are used for fun or by farmers to travel around their farms. Because they weigh little and have chunky tyres, they can travel over rough ground very quickly.

Lunar Rover

Three of the Apollo missions to the Moon actually carried their own car, called the Lunar Rover. Astronauts used these to explore the Moon's surface.

Marion crawler

This massive vehicle was first built to move the rockets that went to the Moon. When loaded, it weighs more than 8,000 tonnes!

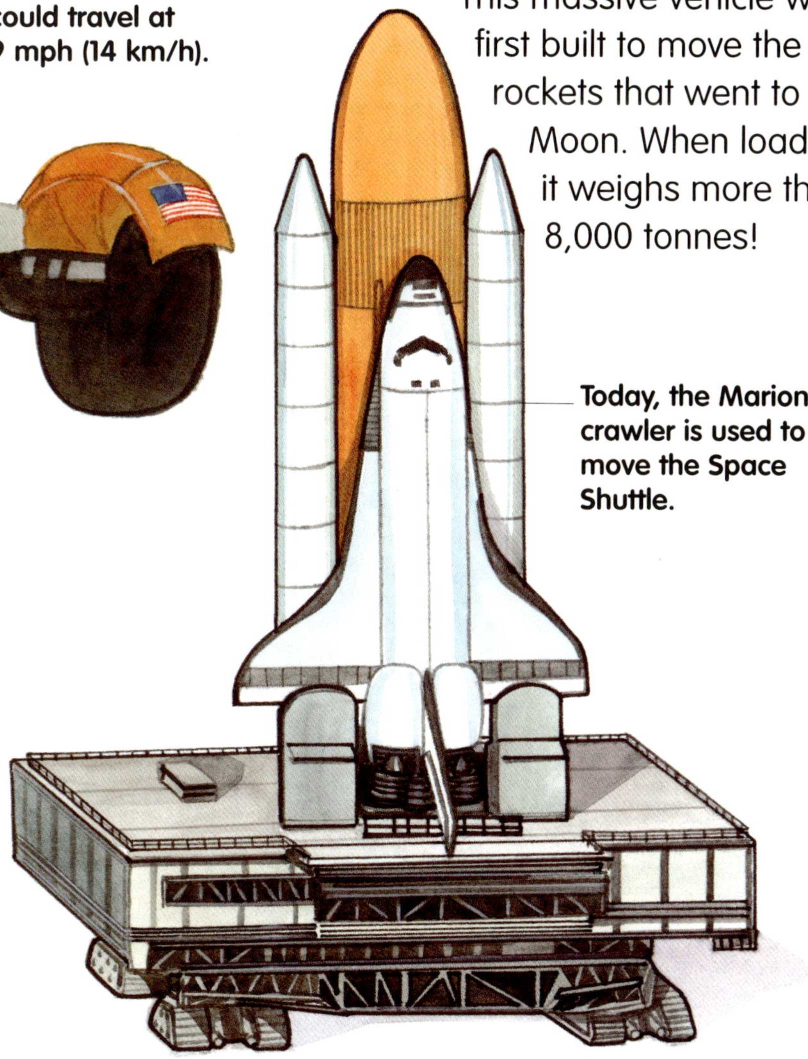

How it works

Some off-road vehicles, such as tanks and diggers, use caterpillar tracks instead of wheels. These tracks stop the vehicle from sinking into the ground by spreading the weight of the machine over a large area.

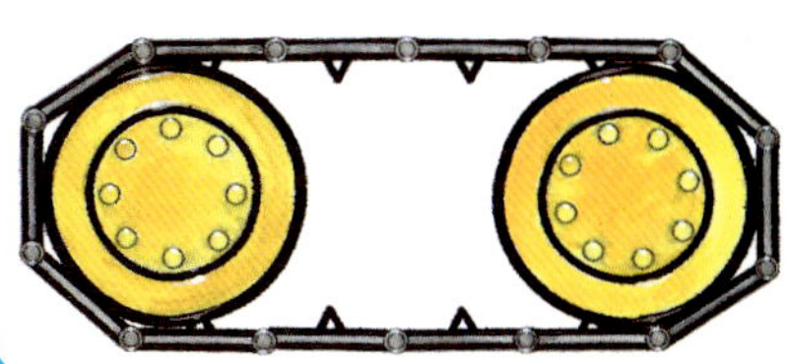

Future land travel

In the not too distant future, we may all be travelling around in very different vehicles. We might have cars that create no pollution, trains that can zoom along at hundreds of miles an hour, or small personal vehicles to drive through crowded city streets.

Electric motors need to be charged before they will work.

Did you know?

Every year, there is a race where solar-powered cars drive for thousands of miles across Australia.

Electric cars

Because petrol-fuelled cars produce a lot of pollution, people have started to look for other ways to power cars. One alternative is the electric motor.

Solar cars

Some people have even been able to build cars that are powered by the sun. These cars do not need any fuel to power them and produce no polluting exhaust fumes. However, these cars are expensive to build and need a lot of sunshine to keep going.

How it works

The body of a solar-powered car is covered in special solar cells. These convert the sun's rays into electricity which the car can use to power a motor. Solar cells are also used to power watches, calculators, and even some homes.

Maglev

This special train actually floats above the ground. A magnet under the train pushes against a magnet on the track, causing the train to float.

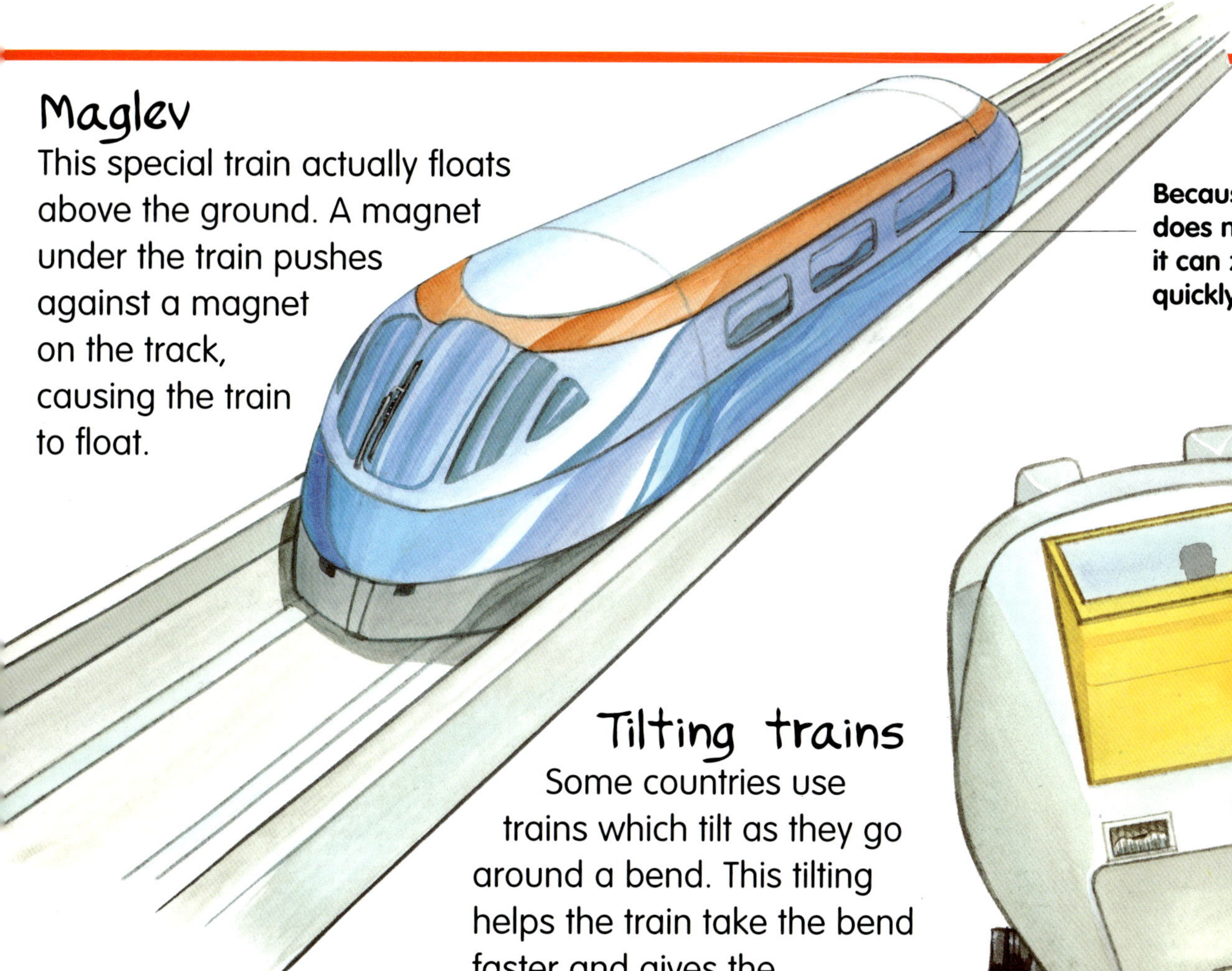

Because a maglev train does not touch the track, it can zoom along quickly and smoothly.

Tilting trains

Some countries use trains which tilt as they go around a bend. This tilting helps the train take the bend faster and gives the passengers a smoother ride.

This scooter has a special roll cage to protect the rider.

Scooters

To get through the heavy traffic in some cities, more and more people are using scooters and motorcycles. These can weave between the traffic more easily than cars. Scooters are also cheaper to run than cars because they use less fuel.

Early sea travel

If you spend a lot of time travelling about, then, sooner or later, you are going to have to cross a stretch of water. This could be a small river, a lake, or even a huge ocean. Some of the earliest people became so good at travelling across water that they could cross the biggest oceans to reach the most remote islands.

How it works

Objects, such as boats, float because they weigh less than the water that they displace (push out of the way). If an object becomes heavier than the displaced water, it sinks.

Dugout canoe

A dugout canoe is made by digging or burning out the inside of a tree trunk. Early canoes were also made by stitching animal skins together over a wooden frame.

Log raft

A log raft is a simple boat that is made by tying together several large logs. This gives a flat, floating platform which can carry people and cargo.

Reed boat

Reed boats are made by tying together lots of dried reeds. These plant stems are very light and, when tied together tightly enough, they can be waterproof.

Kayak

These boats were designed for travelling in the chilly northern seas. They were made by stitching the skins of dead animals together. They had to be made very well to stop them from sinking into the freezing water.

Egyptian barge

The ancient Egyptians used the River Nile to carry goods and people up and down their empire. Archaeologists have even found river barges in the tombs of noble people. The Egyptians believed that they would use barges in the afterlife to carry them across the heavens.

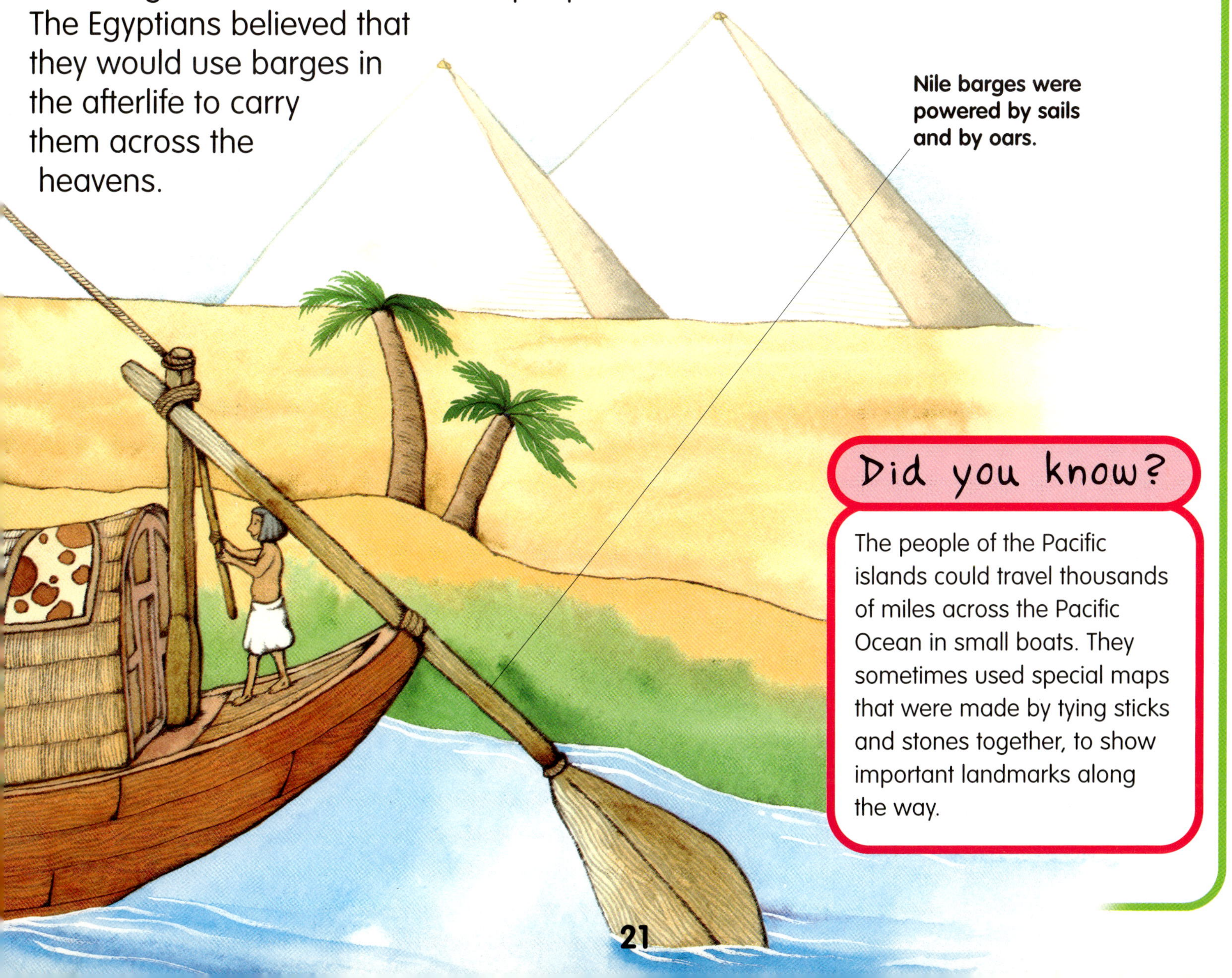

Did you know?

The people of the Pacific islands could travel thousands of miles across the Pacific Ocean in small boats. They sometimes used special maps that were made by tying sticks and stones together, to show important landmarks along the way.

Sails and oars

In the days before engines, people had to rely on the wind to push boats along. However, if there was not any wind, then they had to work very hard, pulling on oars to get the boat moving!

Rowing boat

A small rowing boat uses two oars to push it through the water.

A trireme had three rows of oars.

Greek trireme

The ancient Greeks used boats called triremes. These boats used a great many oars to push them through the water. They also had a sail if there was any wind.

How it works

A sailor unfurls the sails when the wind blows.

Sails work because they catch the wind. The wind blows into the sails and pushes them forward, and the boat with them. If there is no wind, the boat cannot move!

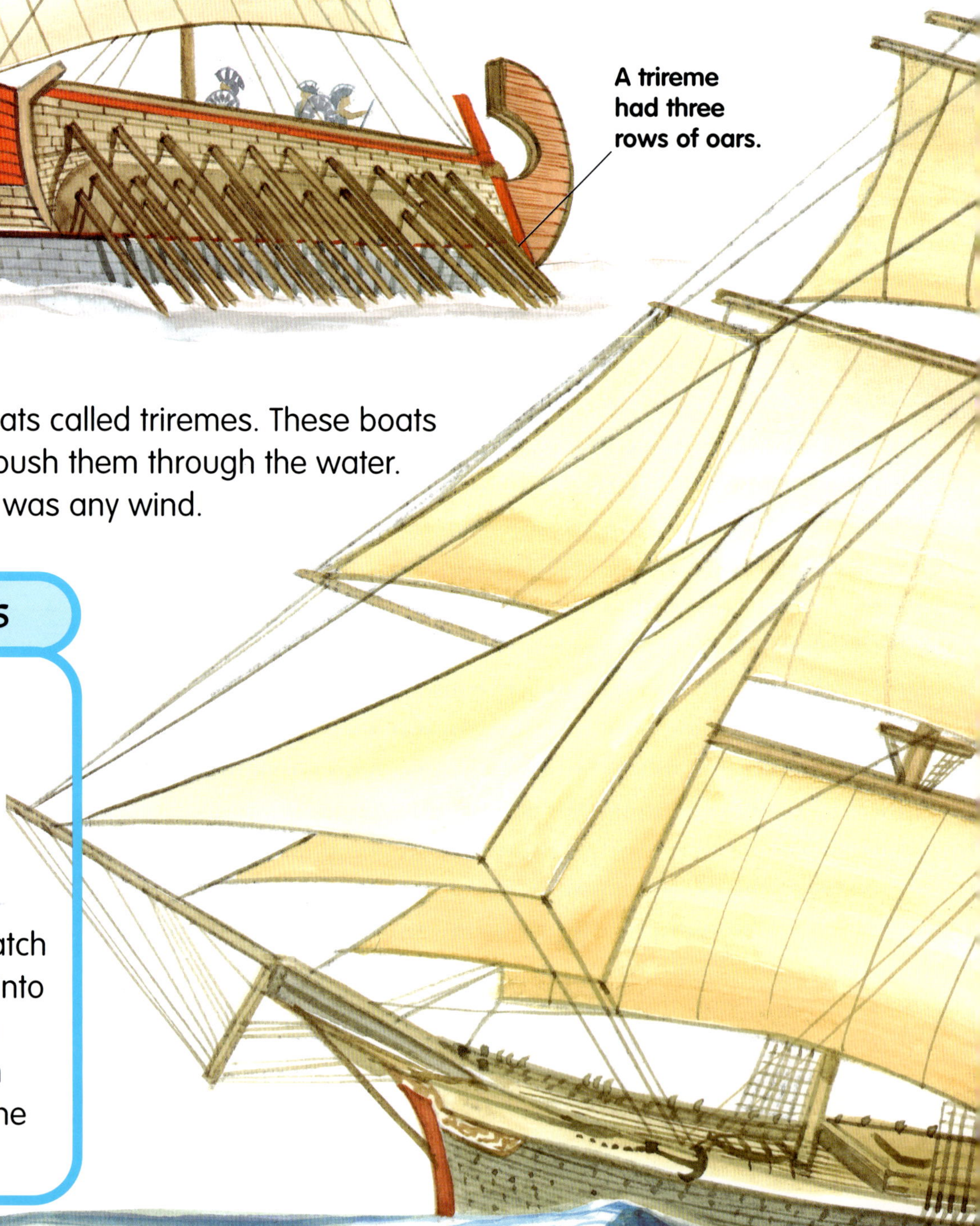

Clipper ships

These ships were the fastest of the late 1800s. They had a great many sails which they could unfurl to catch the wind. They got their name because they could "clip" time off a long ocean voyage. They were used to carry goods all over the world.

Clipper ships usually had three tall masts.

Galleon

These large ships were built over 400 years ago. Many of them were used as warships and carried a lot of cannons.

Arab dhow

These ships have triangle-shaped sails. They have been used for many hundreds of years.

Did you know?

An expedition led by Ferdinand Magellan became the first to sail around the world in 1519.

Paddles and propellers

Industrial developments in the 1800s saw the first boats fitted with steam engines which turned paddle wheels and propellers. Ships were also made from stronger materials, such as iron and steel. However, this still did not stop some of them from sinking.

Iron warships

The American Civil War (1861-1865) saw the first battle between two iron warships, the *Monitor* for the North and the *Merrimack* for the South.

SS Great Britain

The SS (Steam Ship) *Great Britain* was the first ocean liner to be made of iron and driven by a propeller. The ship made its maiden (first) voyage in 1845.

Paddle steamers

These boats had a steam engine which turned one or two enormous wheels to push them through the water. Paddle steamers were very useful in rivers, but rough seas put too much strain on the engine by lifting the paddle wheels out of the water.

Titanic

The engines of the *Titanic* were provided with steam by 29 enormous boilers and 159 furnaces. These could push the ship to a speed of 25 knots. The ship was so well built that it was thought to be unsinkable. Sadly, the *Titanic* hit an iceberg and sank on the first voyage in 1912.

Did you know?

The first steamship to cross the Atlantic Ocean was the *Savannah*. It took 27 days to make the journey. Today, ships can cross the Atlantic in just over three days.

How it works

The propeller on a boat works in the same way as the propeller on a plane, only in reverse. As the propeller spins around, it pushes water back and, at the same time, pushes the boat forward.

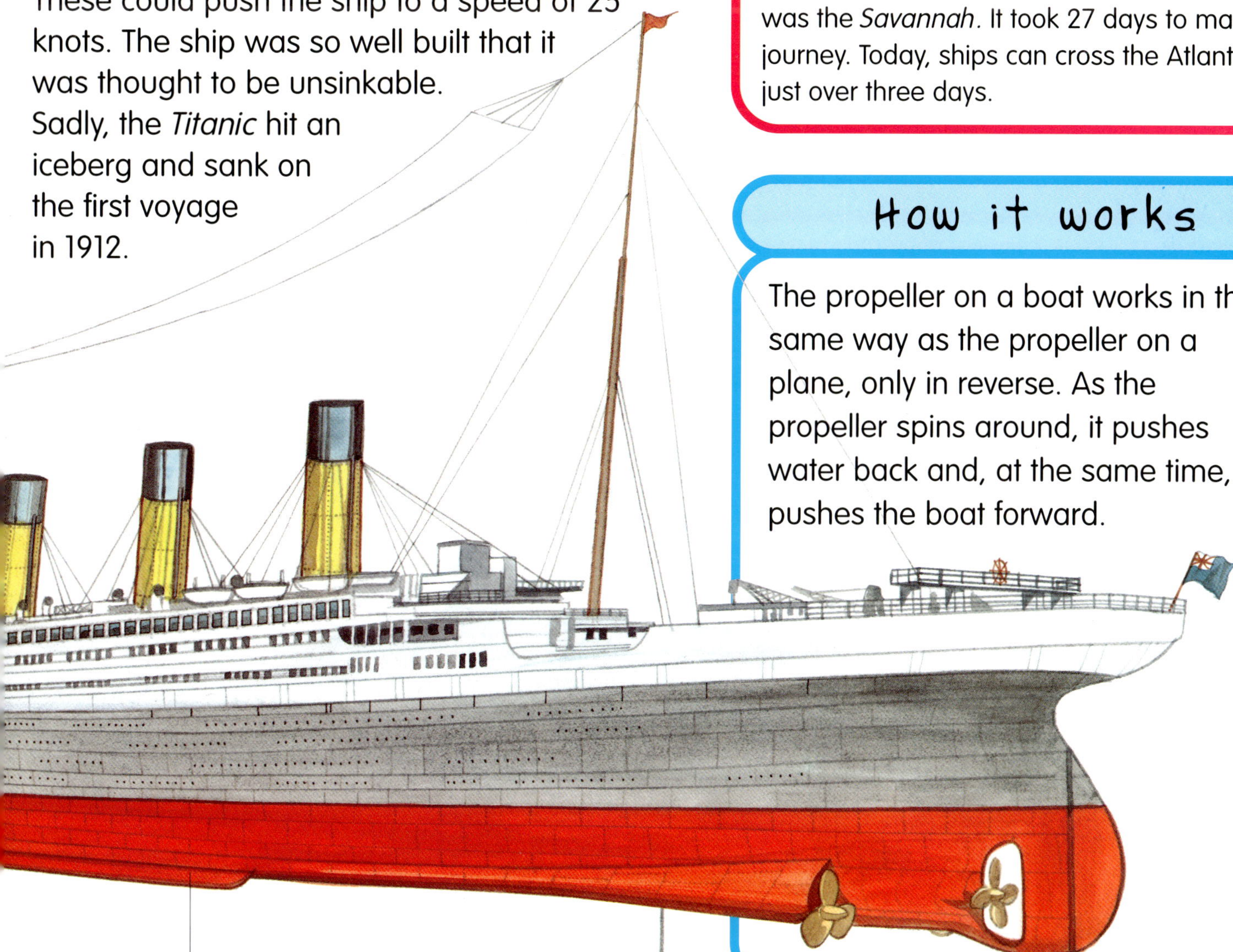

The *Titanic* could carry up to 3,000 people.

HMS *Dreadnought* had a top speed of 21 knots.

Dreadnought

Launched in 1906, HMS *Dreadnought* was the first modern battleship. It had powerful engines and large guns.

Other boats

Today, boats and ships come in lots of shapes and sizes. They also perform a great many roles. They can be small, fun boats, large passenger craft, or enormous aircraft carriers and supertankers.

Jet ski

A jet ski is a small boat which you straddle, like a bicycle. It is used for recreational purposes.

Racing boats

Some racing boats actually trap a layer of air beneath them as they zoom along. This means that they hardly touch the water.

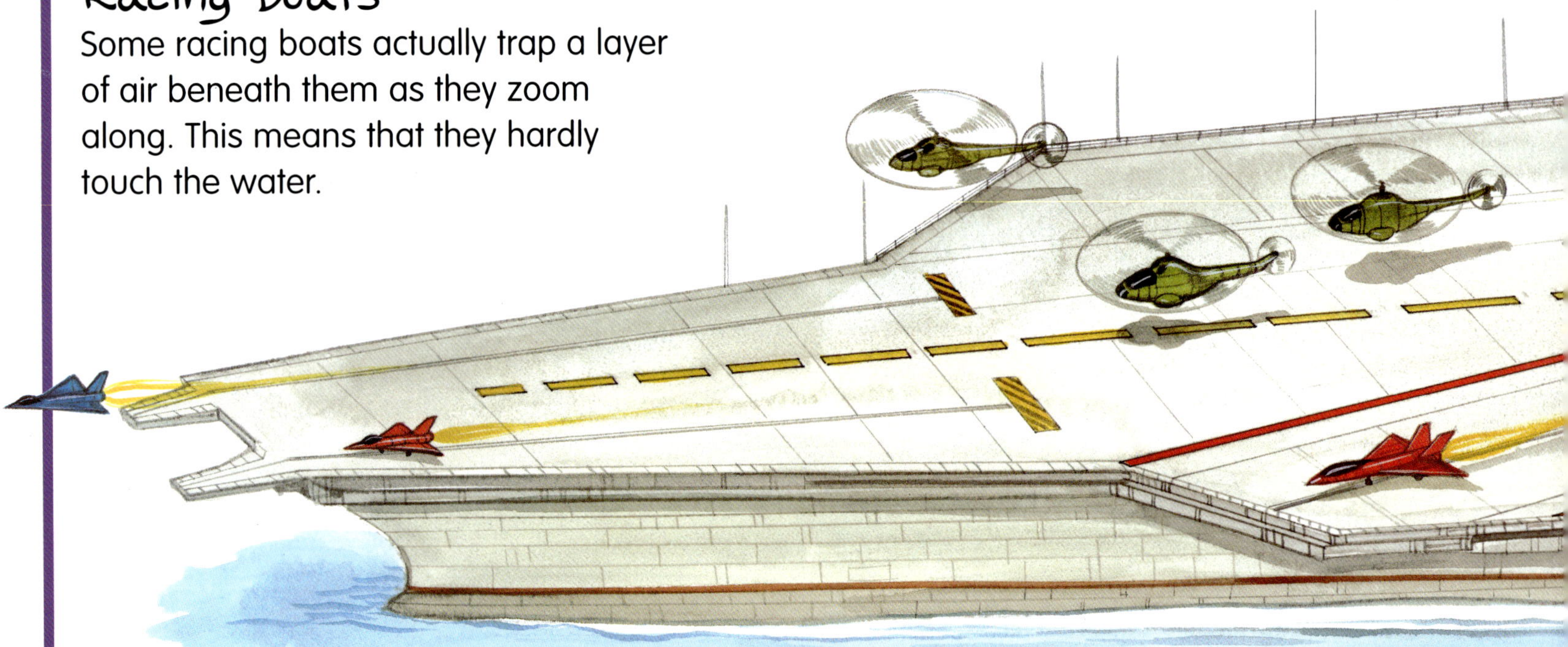

Aircraft carrier

Aircraft carriers are huge ships which carry a number of planes and helicopters. The largest carriers may have up to 90 planes and over 6,500 people on board, including sailors, pilots, and engineers. The planes land on a small runway on the deck and are stopped by arresting wires which catch on a hook at the rear of the plane.

Did you know?

The water speed record is held by a boat called the *Spirit of Australia*. It reached a speed of 511 km/h (276 knots).

How it works

Some boats have special body shapes where they have two or three hulls. They are called catamarans and trimarans. These special shapes mean that less of the boat touches the water. This reduces the friction between the boat and the water, and allows the boat to travel faster.

Oil tanker

The biggest ships in the world are supertankers, some of which can be over 400 metres (1,300 feet) long and weigh over half a million tons! These enormous ships are so big that they need several miles to slow down and stop.

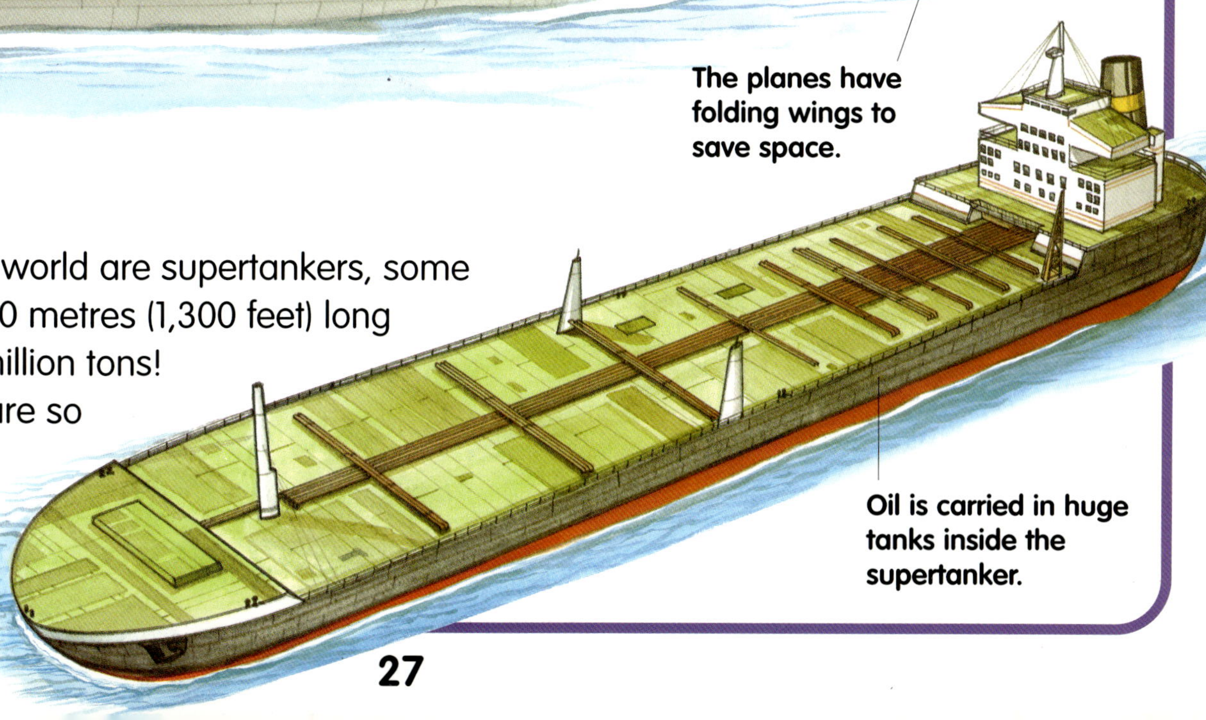

Submarines

Submarines and submersibles are special types of boat that can travel under the water as well as on the surface. Today, they are used to patrol the seas and to explore the ocean's depths.

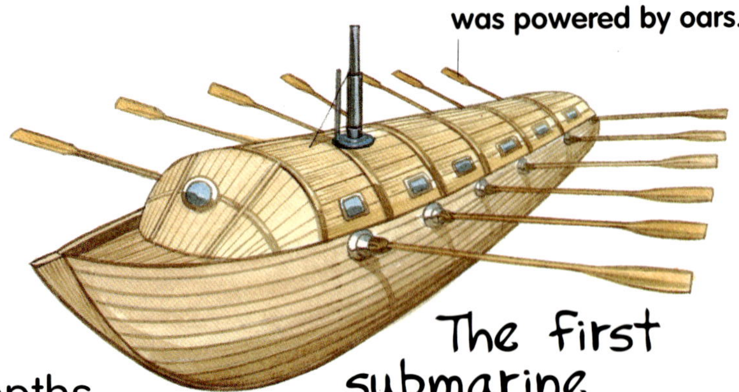

The first submarine

The very first submarine was built by the Dutch engineer Cornelius Drebbel for King James I of England in 1620. It sailed up the River Thames at a depth of 4.5 metres (15 feet).

The Turtle

This early submarine was powered by a single person pedalling inside. It was called the *Turtle* and it was used against a British ship during the American Revolution (1775-1783).

Nuclear submarines

Some modern submarines are powered by nuclear generators. They can stay underwater for a long time, because the generators make oxygen for the submariners to breathe and water for them to drink, as well as providing power.

How it works

A submarine dives under the water by flooding special tanks with water. In order to surface, air is pumped into these tanks. This makes the submarine lighter and forces it up to the surface. A submarine also has horizontal fins, called diving planes, which can be tilted to help the submarine to dive and surface.

U-boat

During World War I (1914-1918) and World War II (1939-1945), both sides used submarines to sink other ships. The Germans called their submarines U-boats, which is short for the German word "unterseebooten".

Did you know?

In 1985, the wreck of the *Titanic* was discovered using a robot submersible called *Argo*.

Mini-sub

This tiny submarine was used during World War II (1939-1945). It was basically a torpedo which was placed underneath a ship and exploded after the divers had swum away.

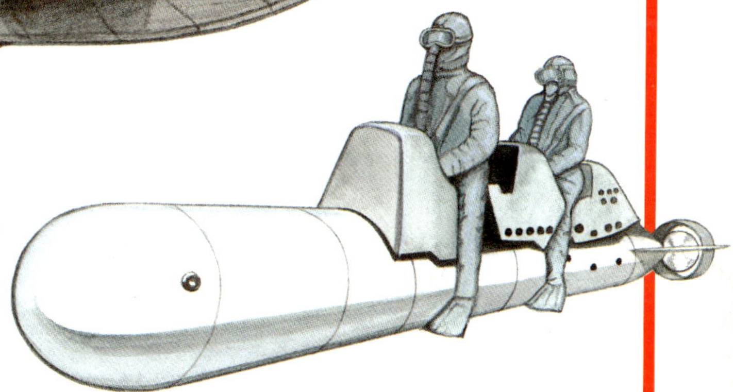

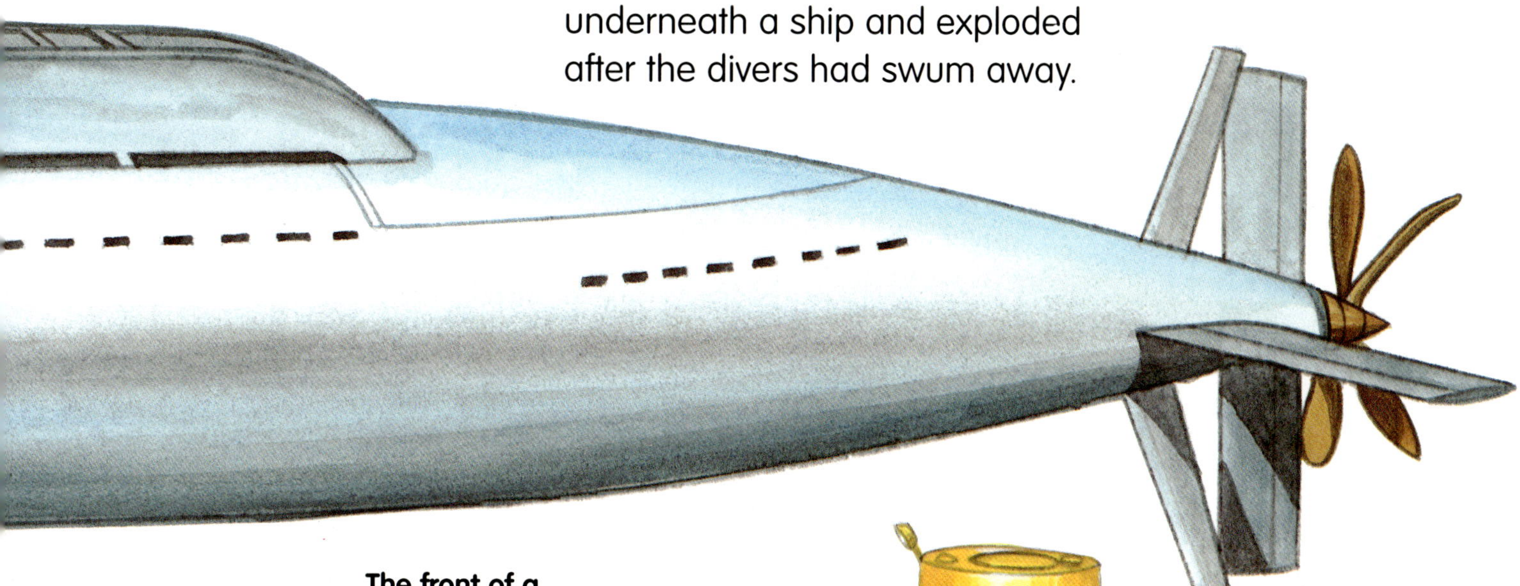

Submersibles

Some vessels are designed to go to very deep depths. They are called submersibles. They carry scientists who want to study what happens on the ocean floor.

Future sea travel

The sea is still largely unexplored. Even the Moon has been mapped in more detail than the ocean floor! The future will see the oceans used more and more with bigger and faster vessels. Some people may even choose to live at sea.

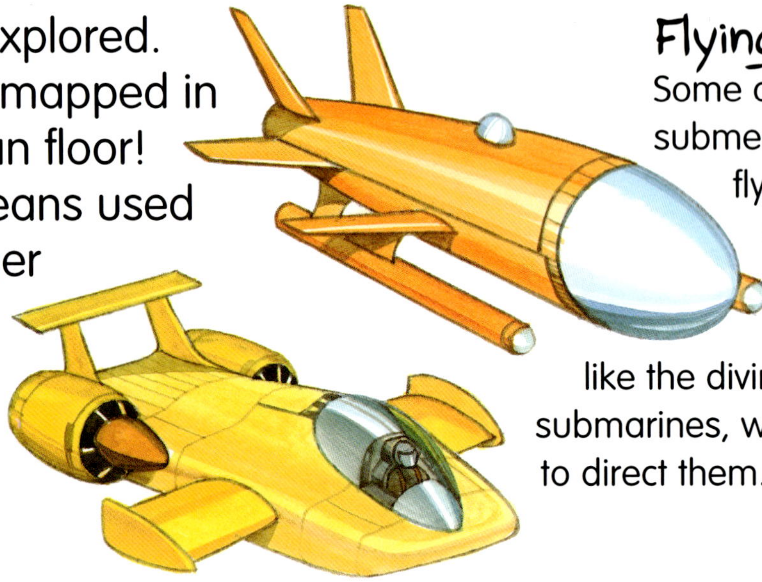

Flying subs

Some of the latest submersibles actually fly through the water. They have short, stubby wings, like the diving planes on submarines, which they use to direct them.

Magnetic boat

This experimental boat is actually powered by magnets. It was built in Japan and can cruise along at 15 km/h (9 mph).

How it works

The magnetic boat has a tube running along its underside. This tube is lined with magnets. When electricity is put through these magnets, water is forced through the tube at speed. This pushes the boat forward like a jet engine.

Floating islands

Plans have already been drawn up for huge, floating cities. On them would be everything for people to live there permanently, including homes, shops, movie theatres, and restaurants.

Stealth ship

Some of the latest warships use stealth technology. They have unusual body shapes and are covered in special paints which make them invisible to radar.

Did you know?

Today, you can spend a whole holiday under the sea, in special underwater hotels.

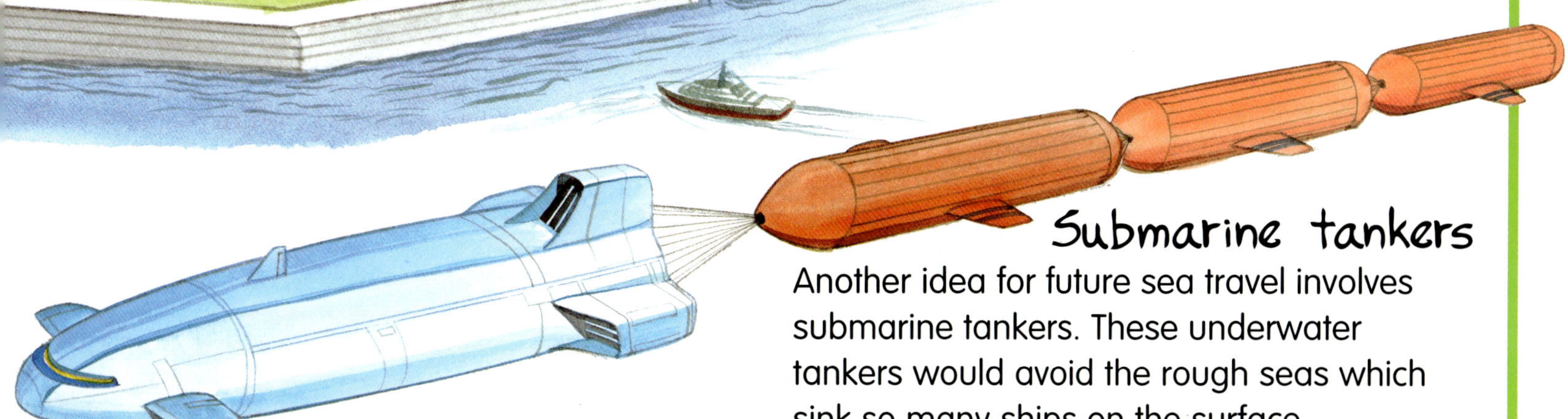

Submarine tankers

Another idea for future sea travel involves submarine tankers. These underwater tankers would avoid the rough seas which sink so many ships on the surface.

Early Flight

For thousands of years, people have wanted to fly like birds. Some of the earliest tales talk about people strapping on wings and taking to the air. Since then, many inventors have come up with many amazing flying machines.

How it works

One of the reasons that birds can fly is because they are very light. This is because the bones that make up their skeletons are almost hollow. On the other hand, Leonardo da Vinci's ornithopters would never have been able to fly because they would have been too heavy.

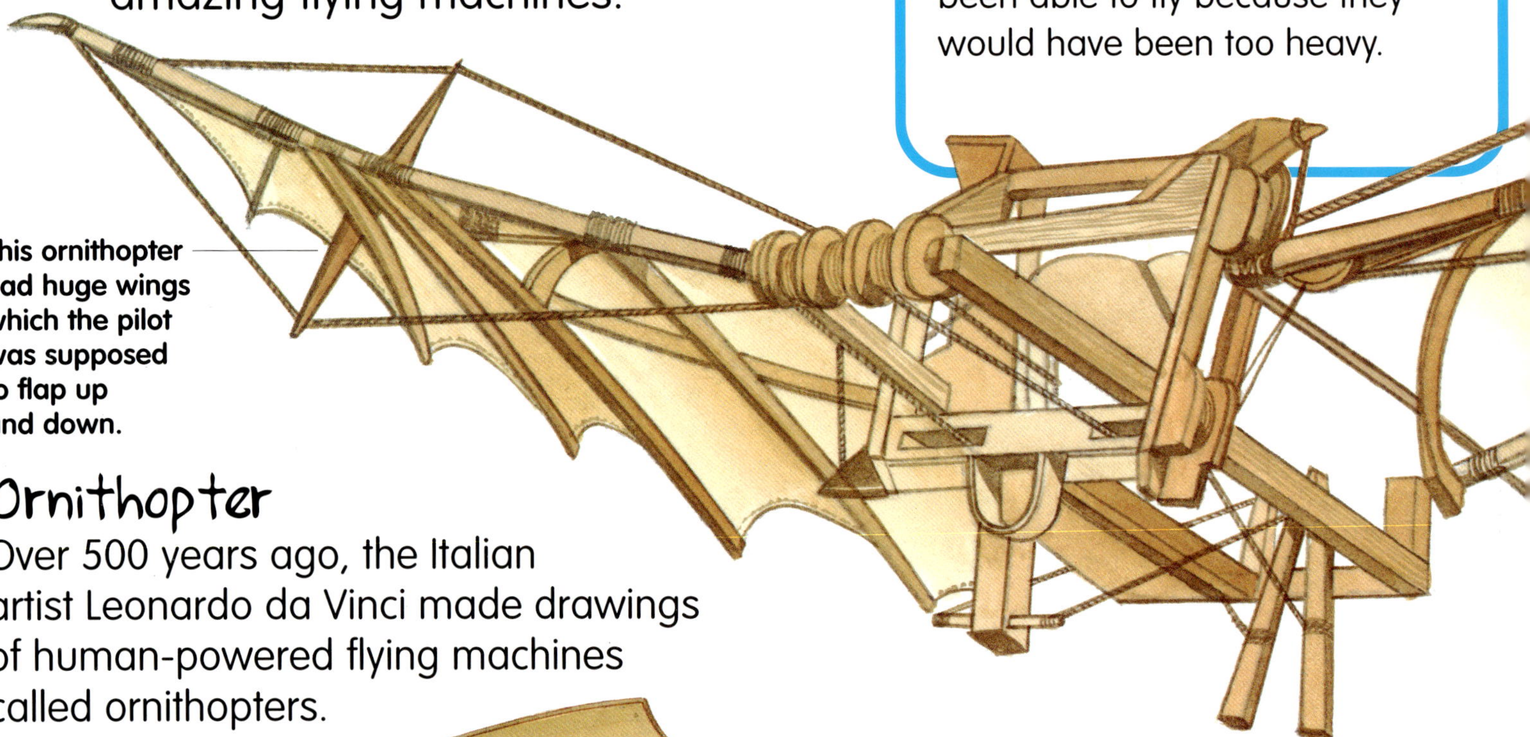

This ornithopter had huge wings which the pilot was supposed to flap up and down.

Ornithopter

Over 500 years ago, the Italian artist Leonardo da Vinci made drawings of human-powered flying machines called ornithopters.

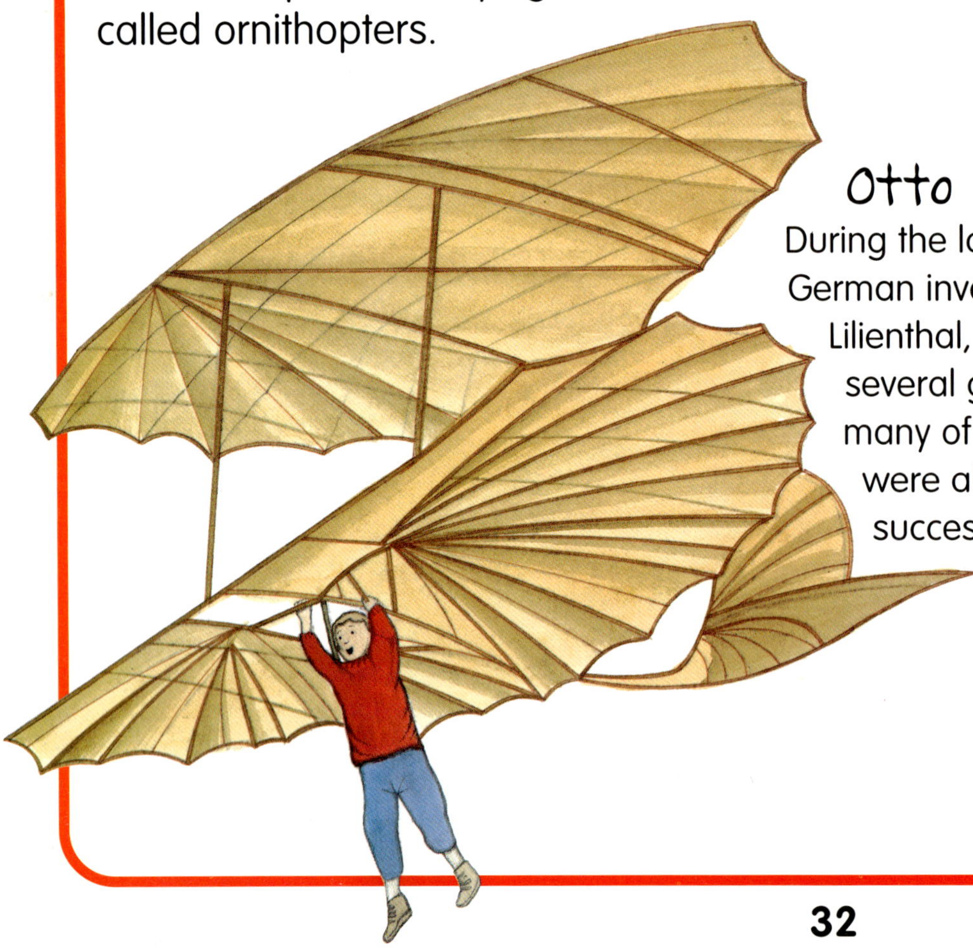

Otto Lilienthal

During the late 1800s, a German inventor, Otto Lilienthal, built several gliders, many of which were able to fly successfully.

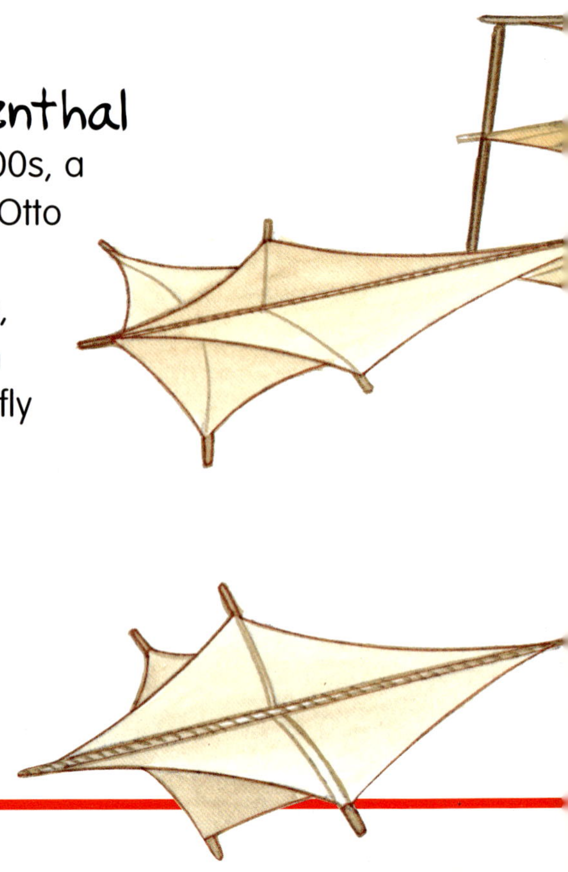

Did you know?

One early design for a flying machine involved a flock of geese that were tied to a carriage!

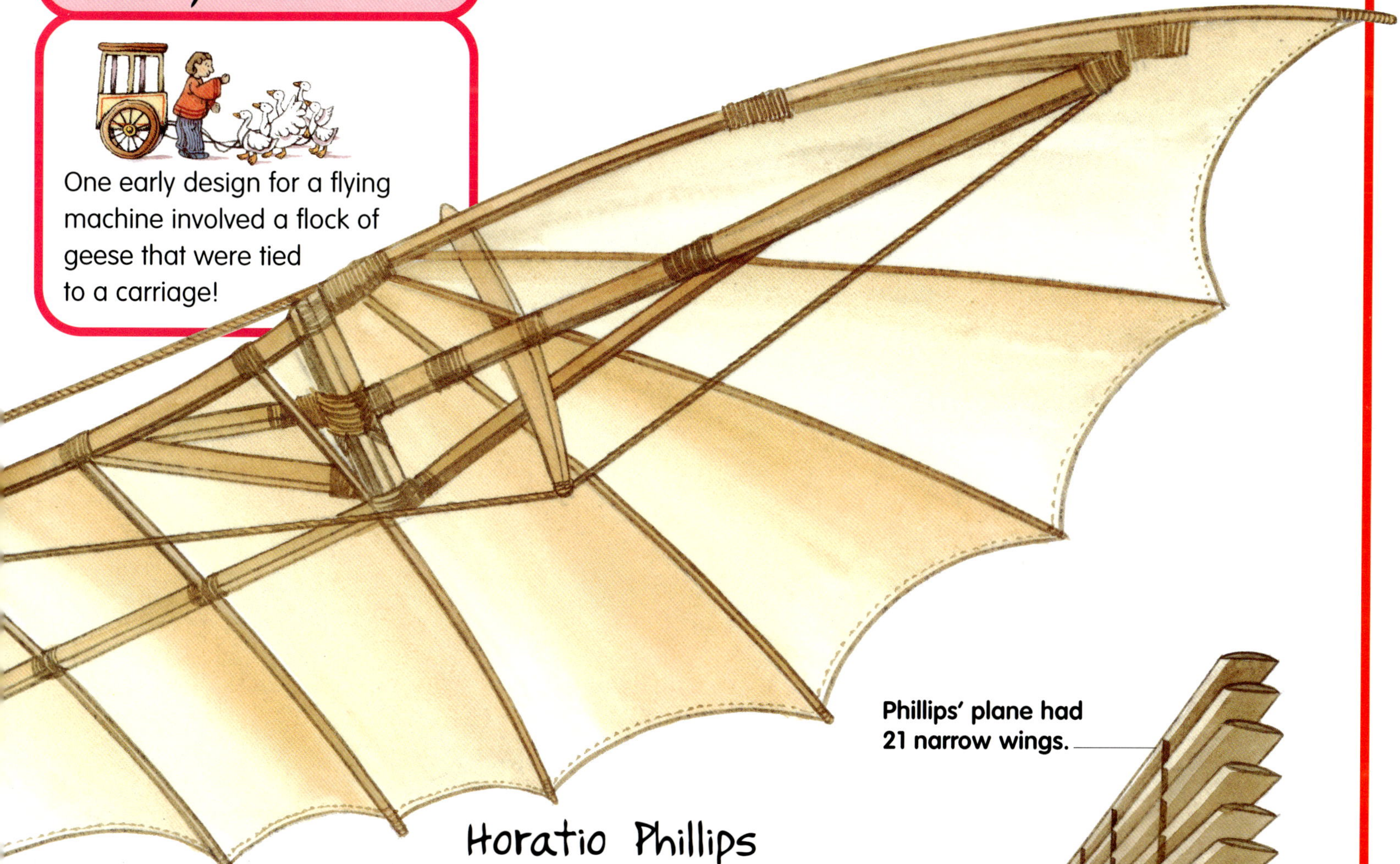

Horatio Phillips

An English inventor, Horatio Phillips, built this strange looking plane in 1904. He claimed that it once flew for 150 metres (500 feet), but this was never proved.

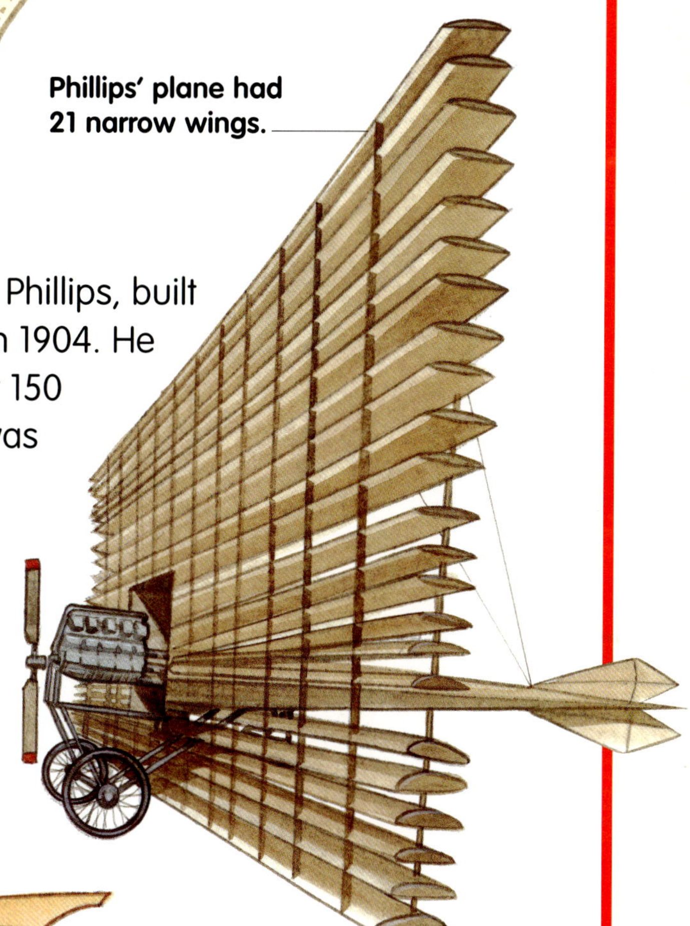

Phillips' plane had 21 narrow wings.

George Cayley

George Cayley was a British engineer and inventor. In 1853, he built the first glider that could carry a person.

Balloons and airships

Ballooning is the oldest form of flying. People have been filling the sky with bright balloons for over 300 years. While balloons rely on the wind to steer them, airships have propellers and engines to push them along.

Early airship

The earliest airships were pedal-powered because there were no engines that were light enough.

Montgolfier brothers

In 1783, French brothers, Jacques and Joseph Montgolfier, built the first hot-air balloon. It was made out of linen and paper and the air inside was heated by a huge fire on the ground.

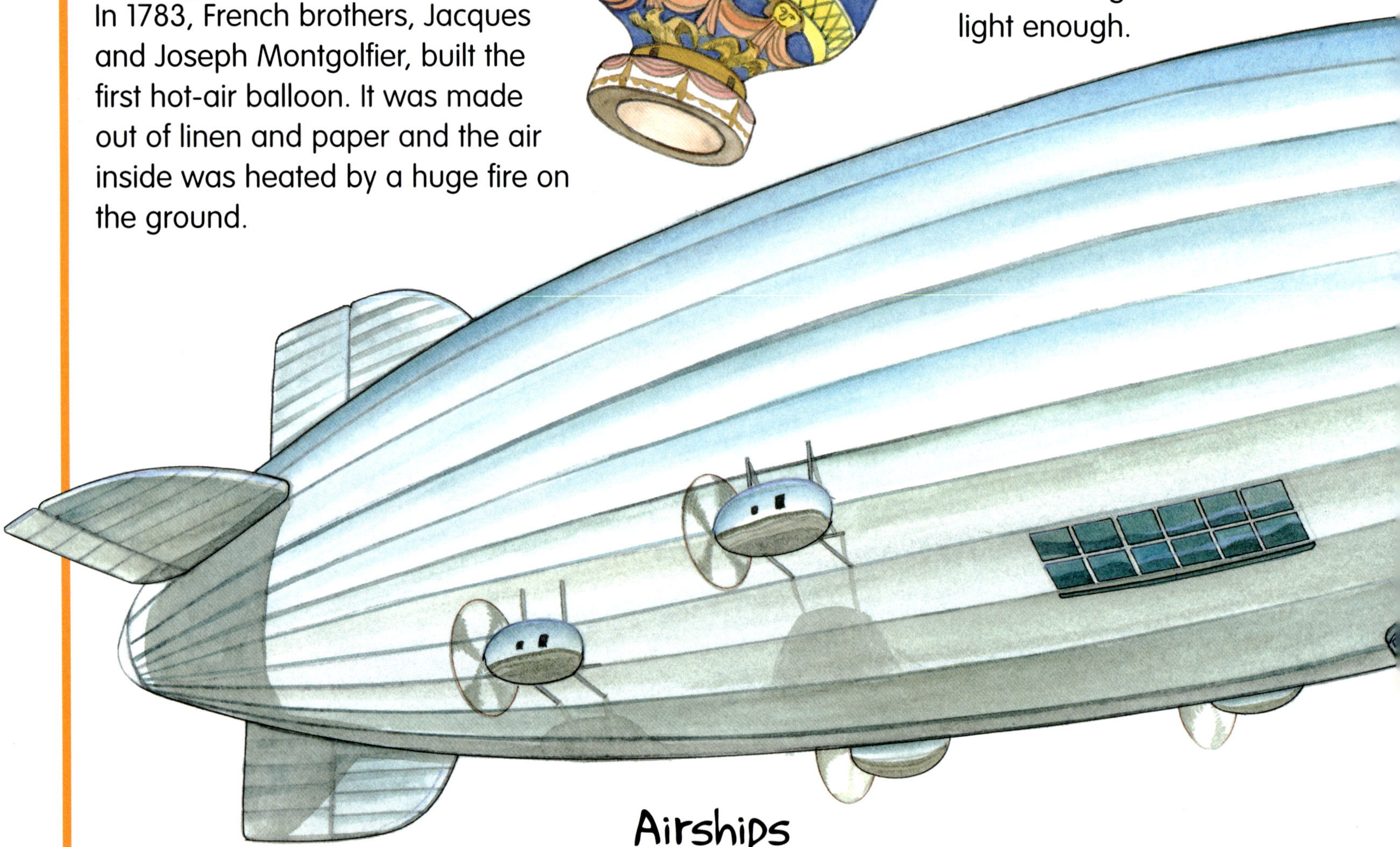

Airships

The great age of airships occurred in the first half of the twentieth century. Huge airships were used to carry people over thousands of miles. However, their use was stopped after a series of accidents to airships, including the Hindenburg and the R101.

Did you know?

Before they let people on their balloon, the Montgolfier brothers tested it by using a sheep, a hen, and a duck.

How it works

Balloons and airships work on the same principle. Balloons usually heat up air inside them using a burner. Airships usually have huge bags of special gases, either helium or hydrogen, which make them lighter than air and able to fly.

Modern balloons

Today, hot-air balloons can come in all shapes and sizes, from small balloons for one person, to enormous balloons shaped like an ice cream.

Long-distance balloons

Some people have flown hot-air balloons over great distances. A few have even managed to fly around the world! These balloons need to travel very high to make use of fast winds called jetstreams.

Modern airship

Because hydrogen is thought to have caused many explosions on airships, modern airships use a gas called helium.

The pilot on an airship sits in the gondola.

Biplanes and triplanes

Compared to today's aircraft, early planes look very different. Many of the earliest planes needed several wings to help get them off the ground. Planes with two wings were called biplanes and planes with three wings were called triplanes.

Louis Bleriot

The French pilot, Louis Bleriot, became the first person to fly across the English Channel in 1909.

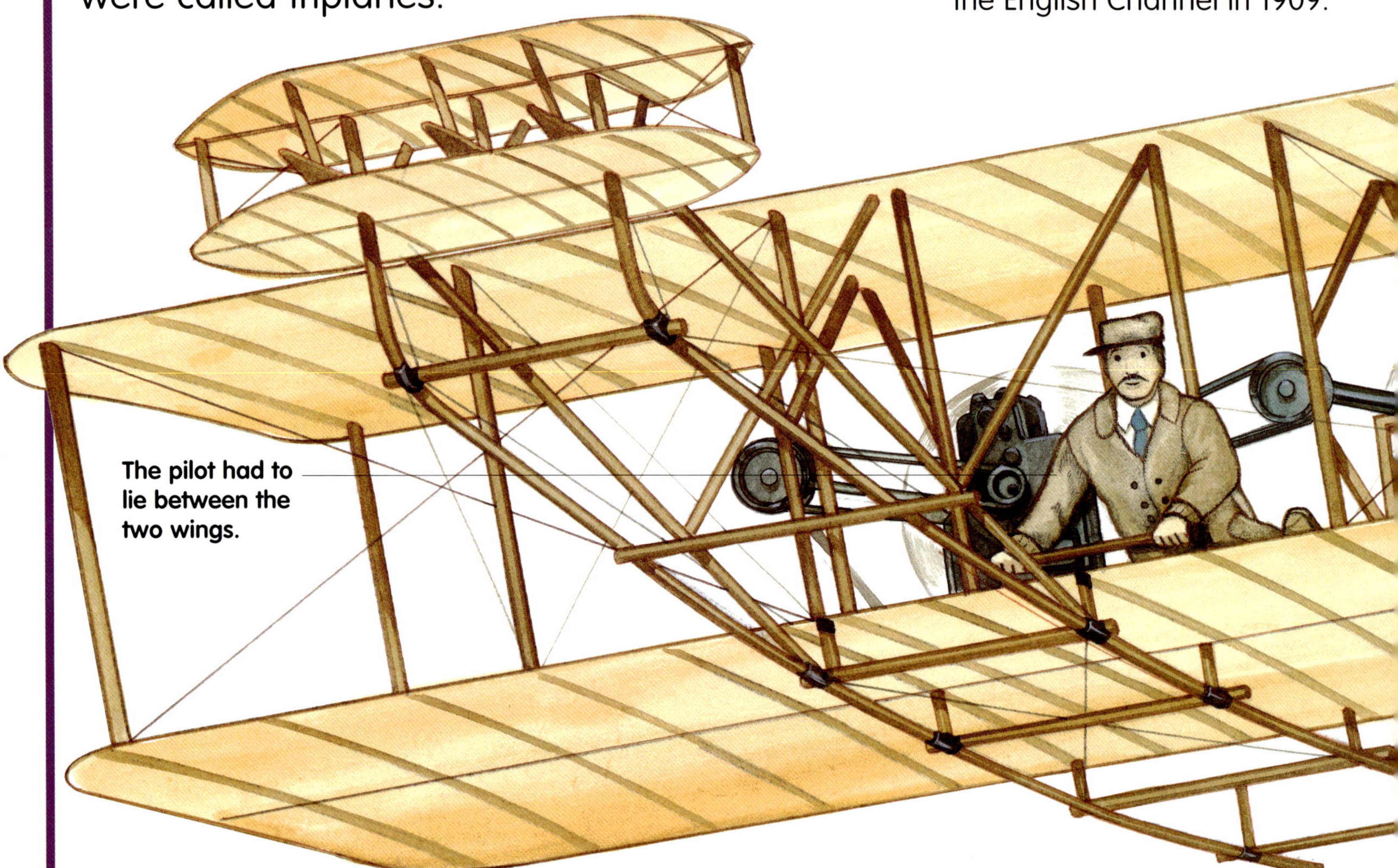

How it works

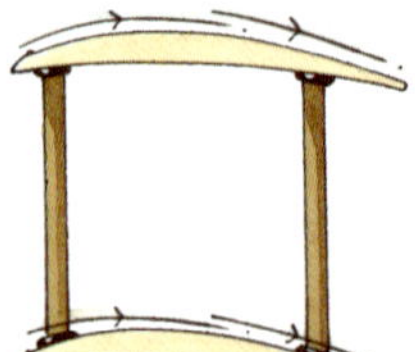

A wing has a special shape. Air going over the wing moves faster and has less pressure than air below it. This lifts the wing and the plane with it.

Wright Brothers

In 1903, Wilbur and Orville Wright built and flew the world's first powered, controllable plane. The first flight lasted just 12 seconds across the sands at Kitty Hawk, North Carolina, USA.

Did you know?

When Alcock and Brown flew across the Atlantic, they had to walk out onto the wings to knock ice off.

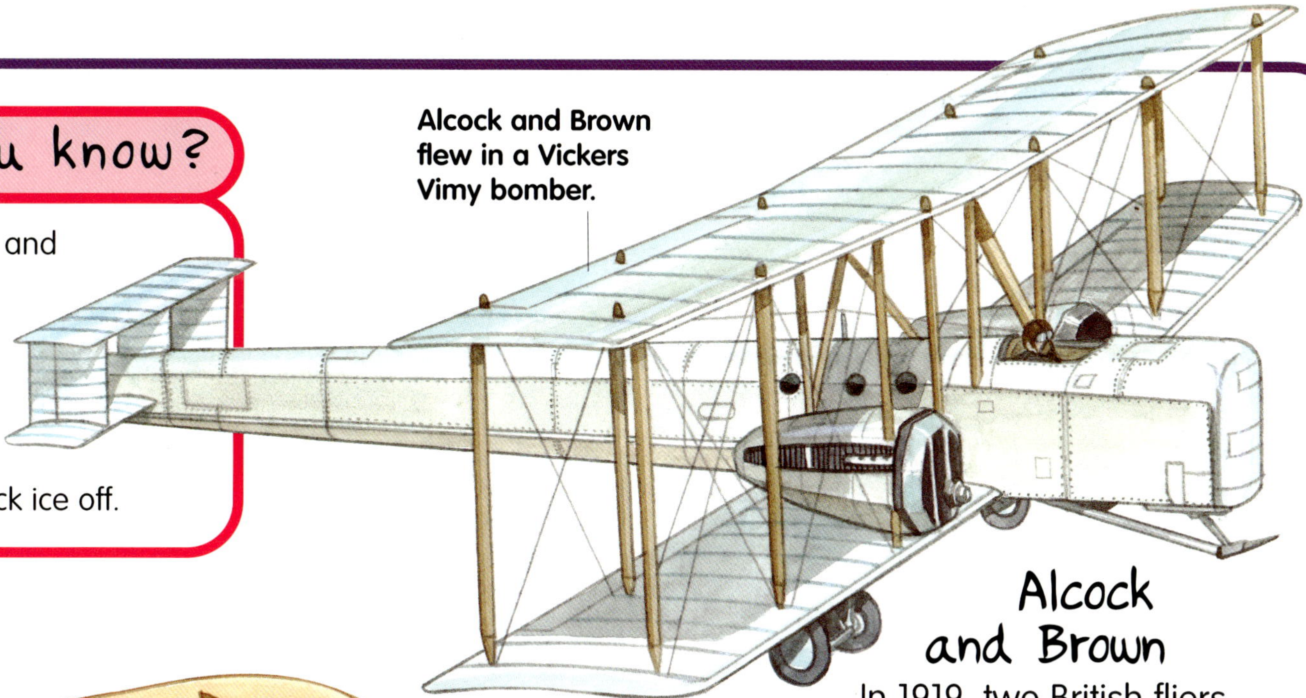

Alcock and Brown

In 1919, two British fliers, John Alcock and Arthur Brown, made the first non-stop flight across the Atlantic.

Wingwalkers

In the early days of flying, wingwalking was a common way of entertaining people at airshows. A person would walk out onto the wing and wave at the crowds as the planes flew by.

First airlines

Not long after the end of World War I (1914-1918), the first airlines appeared, carrying people around the world. At first, they flew converted bombers, but later used planes specially built to carry passengers, such as this Handley Page HP42.

Propeller power

The earliest planes were all driven by fast-spinning blades called propellers. You can still see some planes with propellers today.

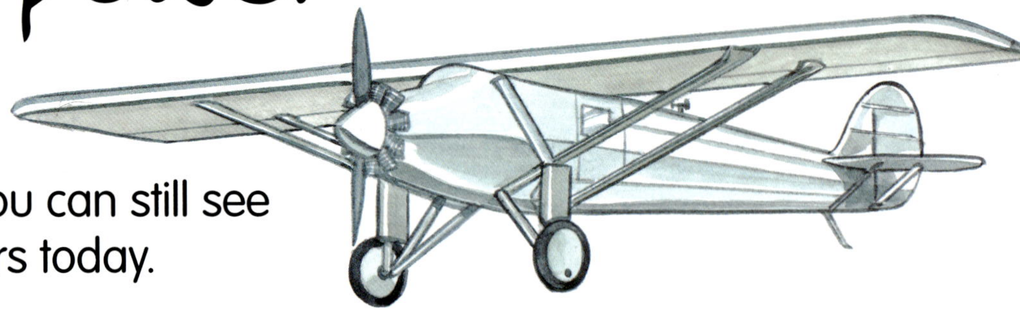

Spirit of St. Louis

In 1927, Charles Lindbergh became the first person to fly solo across the Atlantic Ocean. His silver plane was called the *Spirit of St. Louis*.

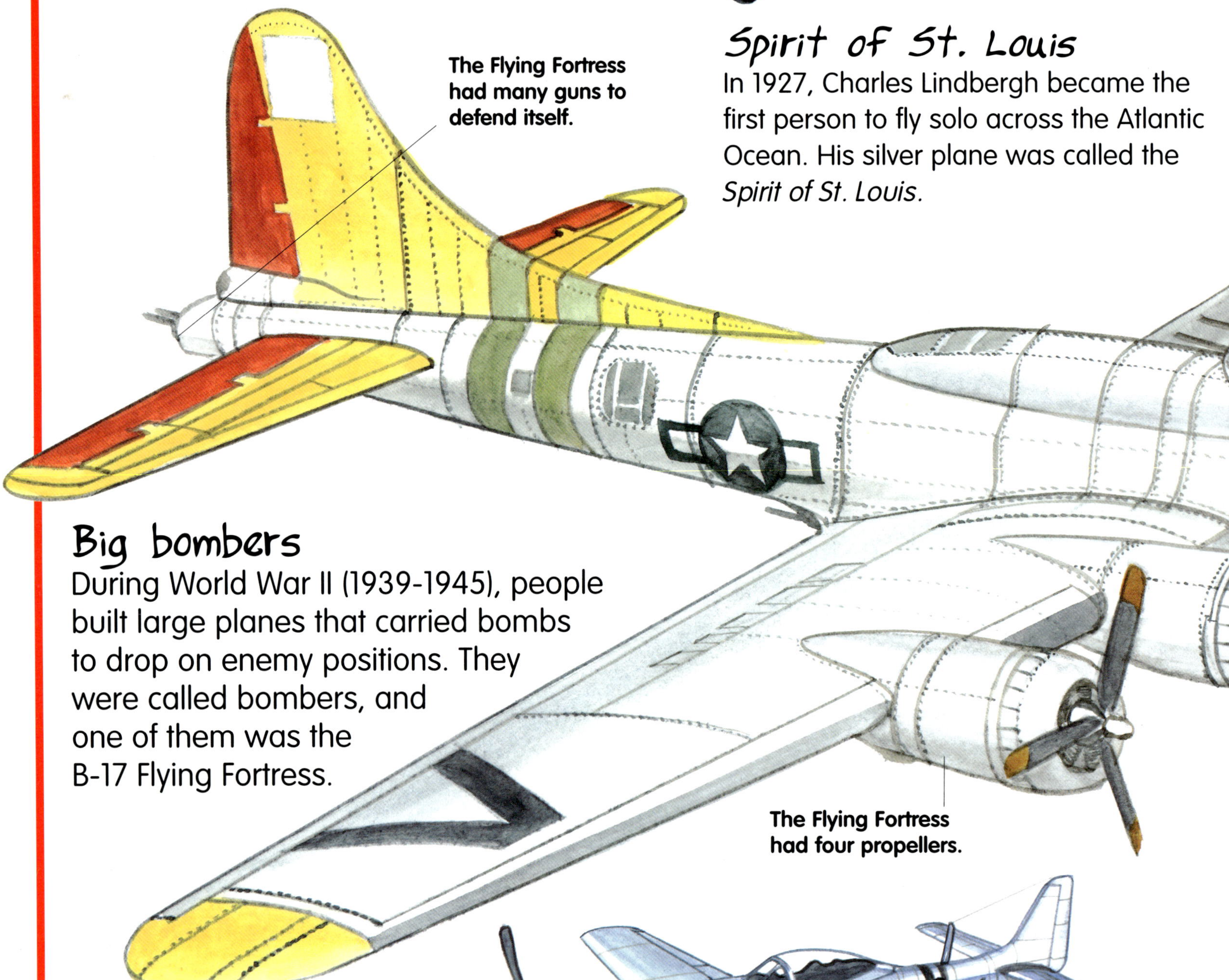

Big bombers

During World War II (1939-1945), people built large planes that carried bombs to drop on enemy positions. They were called bombers, and one of them was the B-17 Flying Fortress.

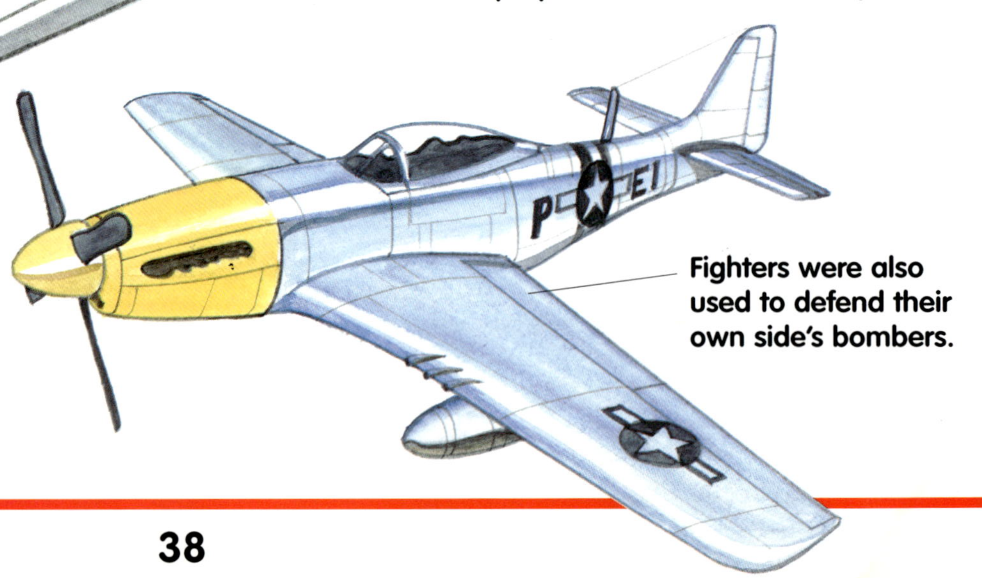

Fast fighters

As well as bombers, people also built smaller fighter planes, such as the P-51 Mustang. These fast planes attacked enemy bombers.

Did you know?

During some of his flight, Charles Lindbergh talked to a fly in his cockpit to stop himself from falling asleep.

How it works

Propellers work by spinning very fast. As the blades of the propeller spin around, they push air behind the aircraft. As the air is pushed backwards, so the plane is pushed forwards. When the plane travels fast enough, it lifts off the ground and flies.

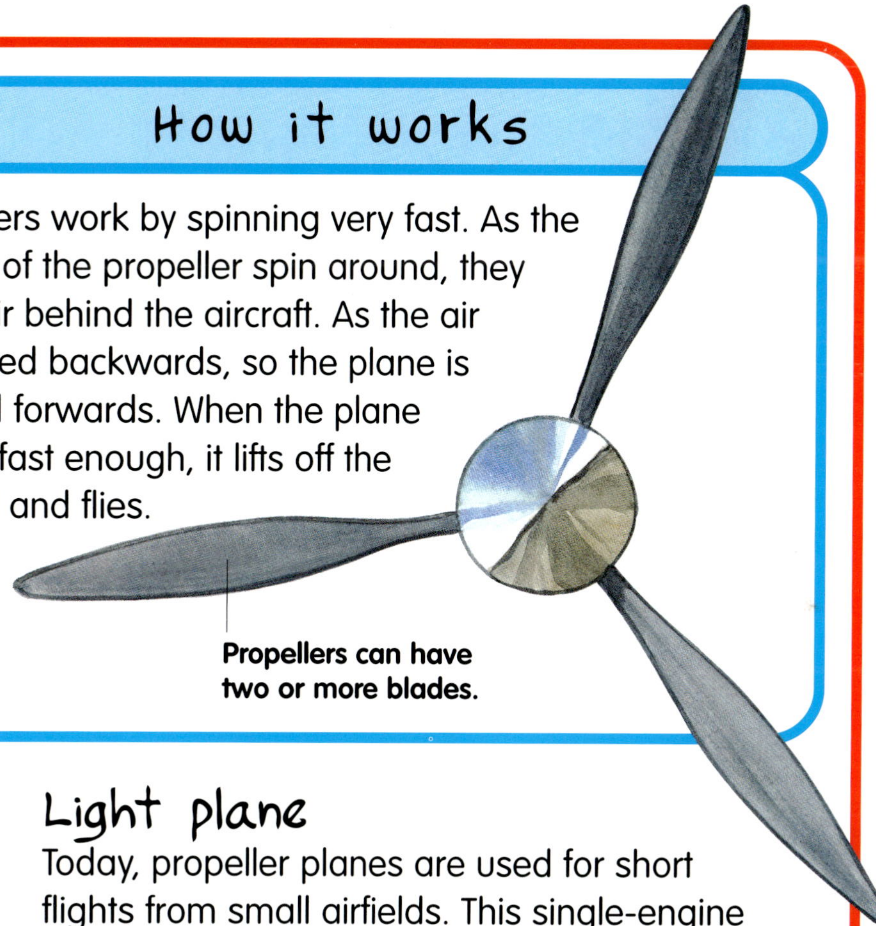

Propellers can have two or more blades.

Light plane

Today, propeller planes are used for short flights from small airfields. This single-engine propeller plane can carry up to four people.

Passenger plane

Larger propeller planes are sometimes used in city airports because they are quieter than jet planes and will not disturb people living nearby.

This passenger plane can carry more than 50 people.

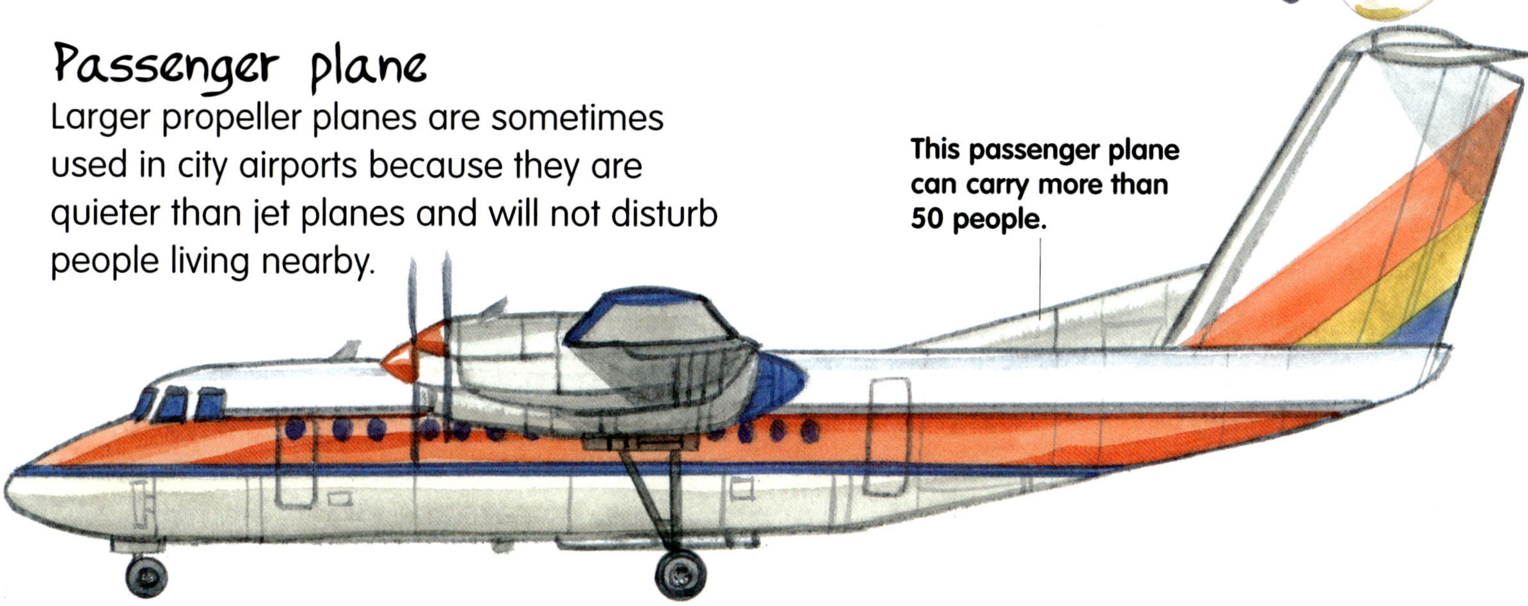

Jets

Jet planes have only been around for the last 60 years or so. In that time, they have generally replaced propeller engines on larger aircraft and now push planes farther, higher, and faster than ever before.

Early jets

The first jet planes appeared just before World War II (1939-1945). This German fighter, a Messerschmidt 262, was called the "swallow" because of its swept-back wings.

Concorde

Concorde is the fastest passenger aircraft in the world. It can fly at twice the speed of sound and at a height of 18,000 metres (59,000 feet), and can cross the Atlantic in just over three hours.

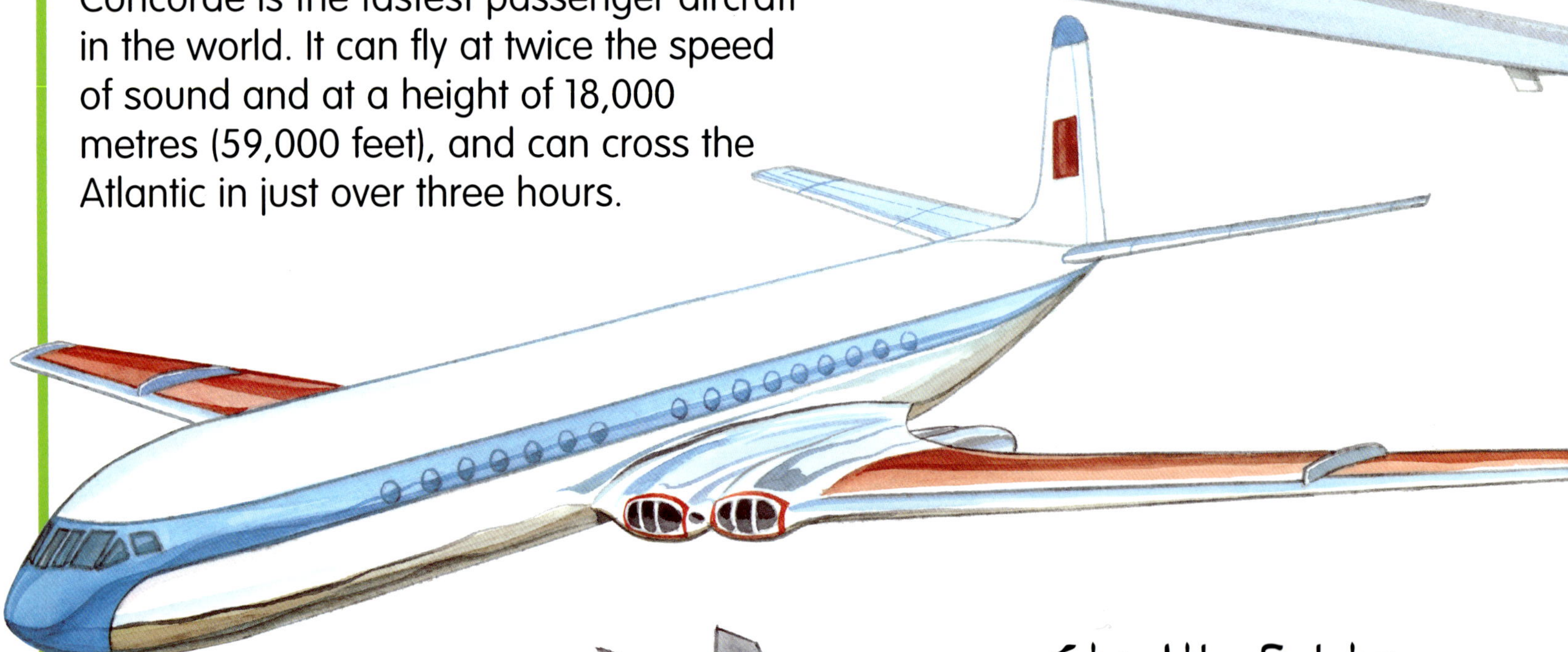

Passenger jets

The first jet airliner was the De Haviland Comet. Its first passenger flight was in 1952. Since then, thousands of jet airliners have been built to carry people all over the world.

Stealth fighter

The funny shape of this jet plane actually makes it invisible to radar. This allows the plane to attack enemy positions without being spotted.

Hovering plane

The Harrier jump-jet can take off and land vertically and hover in mid-air. It can take off from a small forest clearing or from the deck of a small ship.

These movable nozzles allow the Harrier to hover.

Did you know?

The fastest jet plane was the SR-71 Blackbird. It could reach a speed of 3,530 km/h (2,193 mph). That is more than three times the speed of sound.

Concorde has a wing shaped like a triangle. This is called a delta wing.

How it works

A jet engine works by taking in air from in front. Fuel is then added to this air and set alight. The hot gases then shoot out of the back of the jet engine, pushing the engine forward and the plane with it.

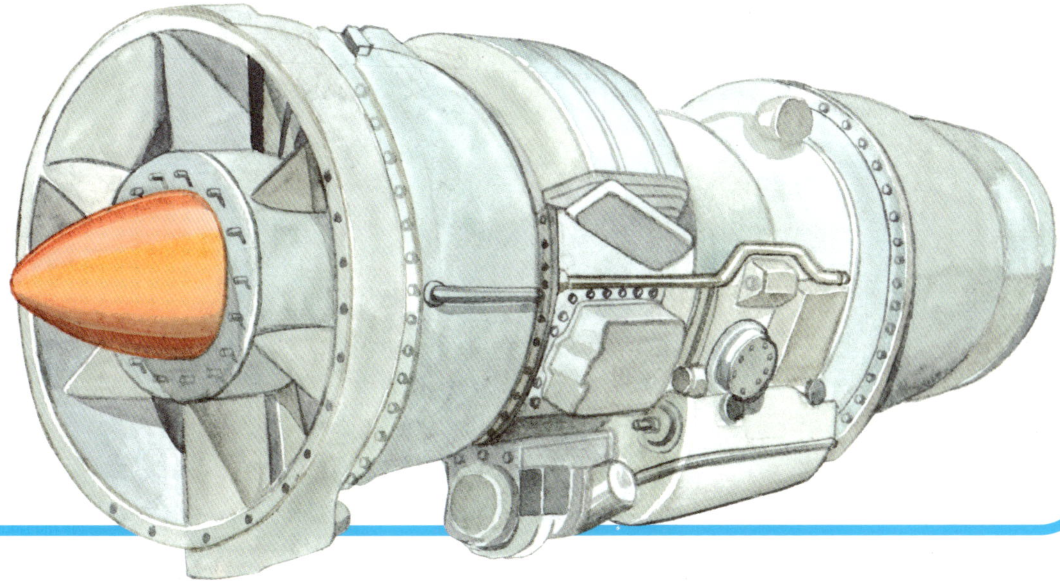

Helicopters

Unlike many planes, helicopters can take off vertically, hover, and even fly backwards! Helicopters are used to ferry people between airports or across cities, carry workers to oil rigs, to patrol battlefields, and as part of the emergency services.

This tail rotor stops the helicopter from spinning out of control.

Leonardo da Vinci

Another of Leonardo da Vinci's designs for flying machines was a contraption that would take off vertically, like a helicopter. He drew this in 1483.

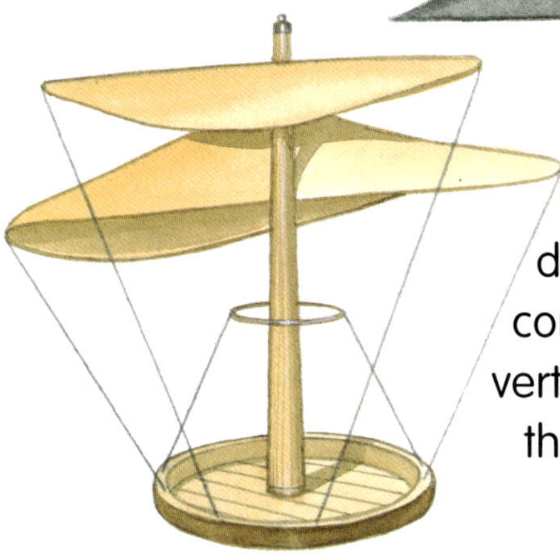

Cornu

Over 400 years after da Vinci made his drawing, the first helicopter took off. This early helicopter, built by French inventor Paul Cornu, hovered for 20 seconds at a height of 2 metres (7 feet).

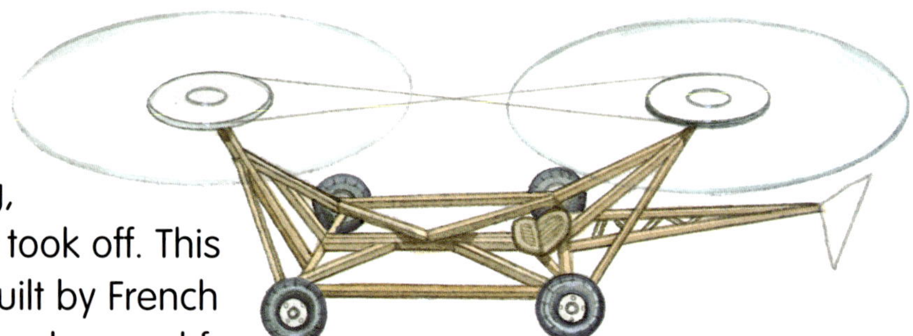

Igor Sikorsky

One of the great builders of helicopters was the Russian, Igor Sikorsky. In 1940, he successfully flew a helicopter called the VS-300. He went on to build a number of other helicopters.

Attack helicopter

Military helicopters have to be fast and mobile. They carry a lot of weapons, including machine guns and rockets. They also have a lot of sensing equipment, including image intensifiers which let the pilots see in the dark.

How it works

The spinning blades of a helicopter work like the wings of a plane (see page 36). As they spin around, the blades create a difference in pressure above and below them. This pushes the blades up, and the helicopter rises with them.

Did you know?

The fastest helicopter in the world is the Westland Lynx. It can reach 400 km/h (249 mph).

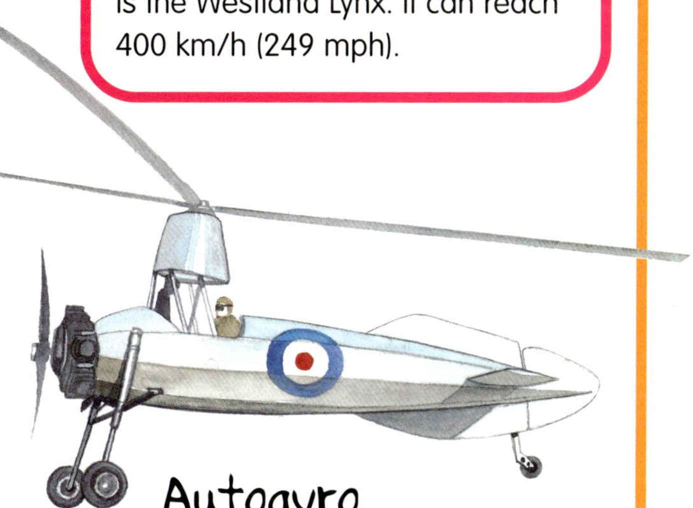

Autogyro

An autogyro may look like a helicopter, but it is different. The large blades on top of the aircraft are not powered by an engine. They spin around as the aircraft is moved forward by a propeller engine.

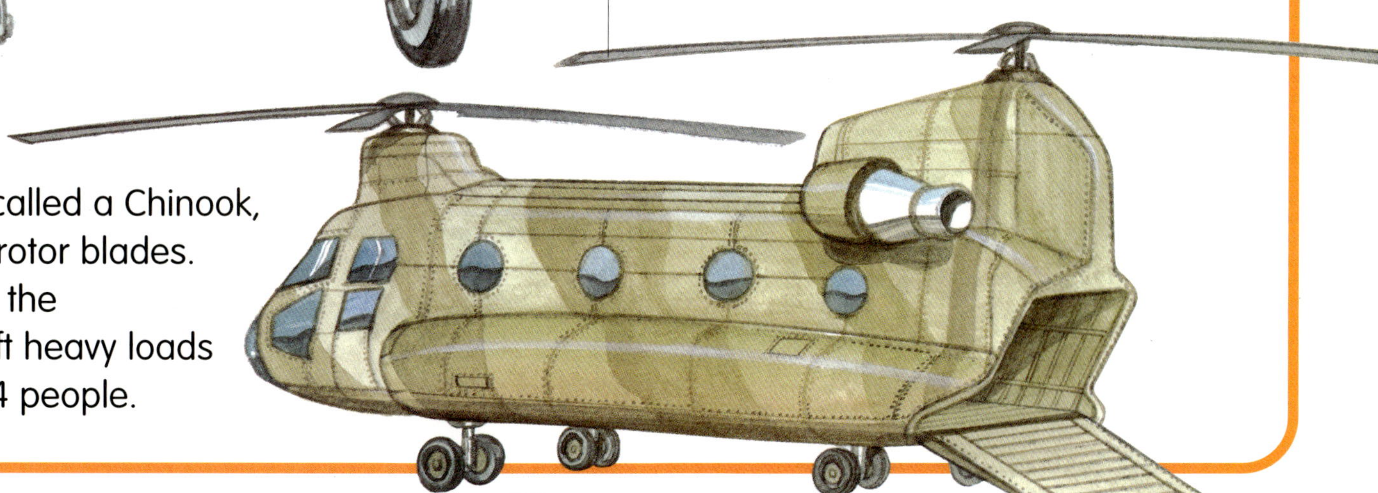

Chinook

This helicopter, called a Chinook, has two sets of rotor blades. This means that the helicopter can lift heavy loads or carry up to 44 people.

Space and the future

People have already flown into space and have set foot on the Moon. The future could see people living in space, faster and less expensive rockets, and planes that can fly themselves.

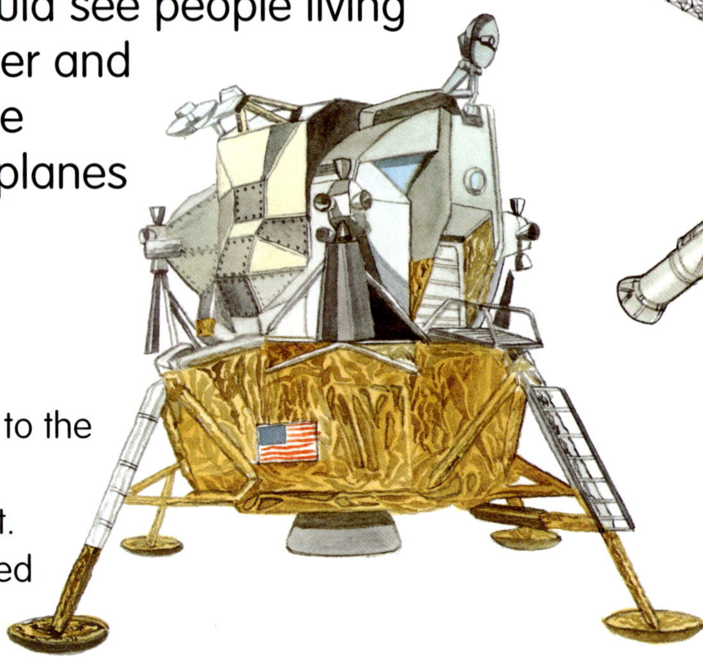

Space probes

A number of probes have been sent to most of the planets in our Solar System. A few, including Voyagers 1 and 2, have even left the Solar System and gone out into deep space.

Apollo

People first went to the Moon inside the Apollo spacecraft. Two people landed on the Moon in the Lunar Lander, while a third orbited the Moon in another part of the spacecraft.

International Space Station

The International Space Station (ISS) will be the largest object ever built in space. It is being built in stages, with the parts being put together in orbit. The ISS will need 44 missions to complete it and, when finished, it will have a crew of six people who will stay in space for three to five months at a time.

Power for the ISS comes from these enormous solar panels.

Did you know?

The Voyager probes carry messages from Earth for any aliens who might come across the spacecraft.

How it works

Rockets work in a similar way to jet engines (see page 40). They also burn a mixture of fuel and oxygen to create hot gases which push the rocket forward. However, above the Earth's atmosphere there is no oxygen floating around, so space rockets have to carry their oxygen with them in liquid form.

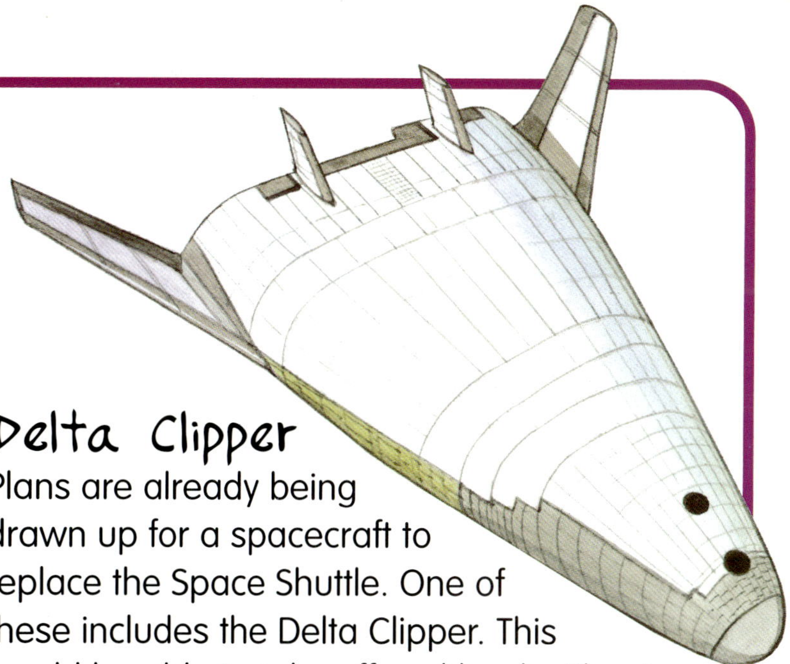

Delta Clipper

Plans are already being drawn up for a spacecraft to replace the Space Shuttle. One of these includes the Delta Clipper. This would be able to take off and land without the need for expensive stage rockets.

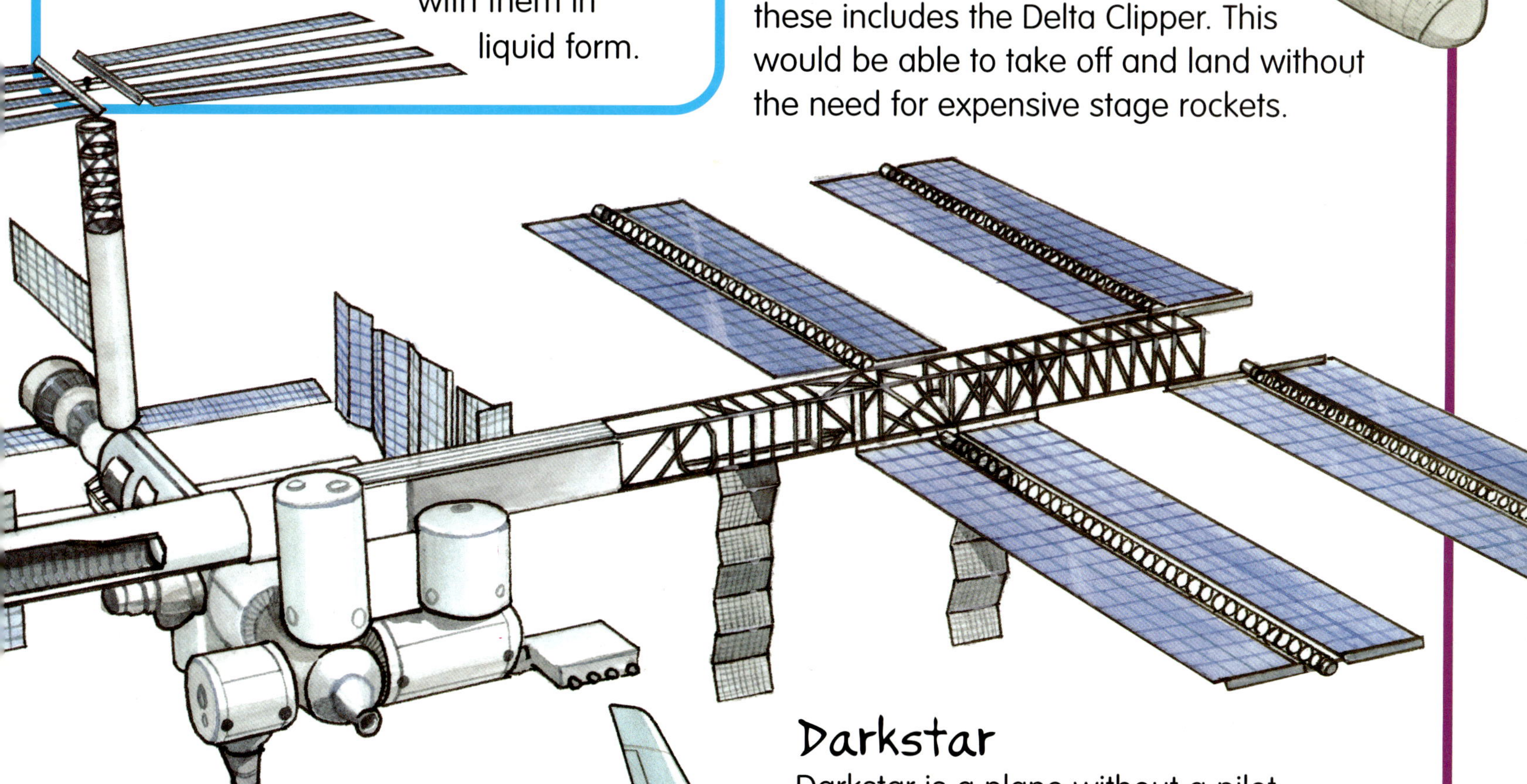

Darkstar

Darkstar is a plane without a pilot. This robot aircraft is used by the military to spy on enemy positions.

Helios

This strange-looking aircraft is powered by the Sun and holds the record for the highest-flying aircraft that is not powered by a rocket. Scientists are using it as a less-expensive alternative to a satellite and to see how aircraft could fly on other planets, such as Mars.

Glossary

Airship
An airship flies because it contains a huge bag of special gases, either hydrogen or helium. These gases are lighter than air and lift the airship into the sky.

Articulated truck
A truck that can bend in the middle is called an articulated truck. It is usually formed of two or more parts: a tractor unit at the front, which holds the engine and the driver's cab, and one or more trailers behind.

Axle
An axle is a bar or rod which runs through the middle of a wheel. The axle lets the wheel spin around rather than drag along the ground. This reduces the friction and makes a vehicle easier to move.

Floating
Floating is the ability of an object to rest on the surface of a fluid, such as water. An object will float if it weighs less than the amount of water it displaces (pushes out of the way). If it weighs more than amount of water it displaces, it will sink.

Helicopter
Helicopters are aircraft that use a large spinning rotor to lift them off the ground. They can take off and land vertically and can even fly backwards.

Hull
The hull is the main body of a boat. Some boats have two hulls and are called catamarans, while those with three hulls are called trimarans.

Caterpillar tracks
These are a series of linked plates that run around a number of wheels. These tracks spread the weight of a vehicle over a wide area and stop it from sinking into muddy ground.

Internal combustion engine
This is an engine where fuel and air are mixed and burnt inside a cylinder. Internal combustion engines are used to power cars, trains, motorcycles, and some planes.

Jet engine
Jet engines suck in air from in front of them and burn it with fuel. This creates a jet of hot gases which blows out of the back of the engine and pushes the vehicle forwards.

Monorail
Not all trains run on two rails. A monorail runs on just one. The train either sits on top of the rail or hangs beneath it.

Piston
A piston is a disc or rod that moves inside a tube called a cylinder. The piston is pushed backwards and forwards by steam in a steam engine or by small explosions in an internal combustion engine. The movement of the pistons is eventually transferred to the wheels or the propellers, causing them to spin around.

Propeller
Propellers are found on some planes and many boats. They have several angled blades which, when they spin around, push the air or water back behind the vehicle and push the vehicle forwards.

Rocket engine
Rockets mix oxygen with a fuel and burn it to create a blast of hot gases that pushes the rocket forwards.

Solar cells
These are special devices which change sunlight into electricity.

Submarine
This is a type of boat which can go underwater. It has special tanks inside itself which can be filled with water to make the submarine sink or filled with air to make the submarine rise.